We are all at various stages of life's journey. Consider this a nautical excursion. Many of you have weathered storms and gale-like winds yet you are still moving toward your final destination. You had great difficulty in giving your craft the correct direction but now you see the buoys associated with the harbor. Your boat is headed in the right direction and the faint outline of the dock appears to be rising through the mist in your field of vision. This brief devotional is intended to be a figurative buoy in your nautical journey of life. Perhaps some of the content might cause you to make some last minute adjustments to your charted course.
May you have safe sailing into the harbor!

I remember the days of old.
I meditate on all that you have done.
I ponder the works of your hands.

I stretch out my hands to you.
My soul thirsts for you like a parched land.

Psalm 143: 5, 6

ESV Bible
Copyright@2008 Crossway
The ESV translation used throughout
this Devotional
Bible verses copied from BibleGateway.com

Table of Contents

AARON

10 But Moses said to the L<small>ORD</small>, "Oh, my Lord, I am not eloquent, either in the past or since you have spoken to your servant, but I am slow of speech and of tongue." 11 Then the L<small>ORD</small> said to him, "Who has made man's mouth? Who makes him mute, or deaf, or seeing, or blind? Is it not I, the L<small>ORD</small>? 12 Now therefore go, and I will be with your mouth and teach you what you shall speak." 13 But he said, "Oh, my Lord, please send someone else." 14 Then the anger of the L<small>ORD</small> was kindled against Moses and he said, "Is there not Aaron, your brother, the Levite? I know that he can speak well. Behold, he is coming out to meet you, and when he sees you, he will be glad in his heart. 15 You shall speak to him and put the words in his mouth, and I will be with your mouth and with his mouth and will teach you both what to do. 16 He shall speak for you to the people, and he shall be your mouth, and you shall be as God to him. 17 And take in your hand this staff, with which you shall do the signs."

Exodus 4:10-17

1 For every high priest chosen from among men is appointed to act on behalf of men in relation to God, to offer gifts and sacrifices for sins. 2 He can deal gently with the ignorant and wayward, since he himself is beset with weakness. 3 Because of this he is obligated to offer sacrifice for his own sins just as he does for

those of the people. ⁴ And no one takes this honor for himself, but only when called by God, just as Aaron was.
Hebrews 5:1-4

When we think of someone being called by God for a specific task, we generally think in terms of a very apparent and specific call as was the case with the apostle Paul being rendered helpless and blind for a three-day period.

We don't really consider that our vocation, our spouse selection, our volunteerism to be a call from God. Yet, with God there are no casual happenings. In fact, each of us has received calls from God that we may have glossed over and not even considered that God was calling us. God's calls could be in preparing us by our choice of educational institution, courses selected, part and fulltime work selection, friend choice, marriage partner etc. As you look back upon your choices, do you see God's guidance?

God selected Moses to lead the Israelites to the Promised Land. Yet Moses attempted to try to weasel out of his calling by telling God that his lack of glib speaking skills should eliminate him from saying yes to God's direct call. So, God in exasperation said "how about Aaron your brother, he speaks eloquently" Aaron received his calling by apparent default.

The lessons to be learned from today's scripture is that when God calls, we need to:

- Be open to the call
- Recognize that it is God's call

- Listen to others that compliment us upon our strengths
- Listen carefully to how God is speaking to us
- Be aware that just because something appears correct, it might not be God's call
- Through prayer analyze God's call

Prayer: Father, give me a discerning heart to recognize your voice. Then, may I act in obedience. Amen

ABIDING

I Am the True Vine

15 *"I am the true vine, and my Father is the vinedresser. 2 Every branch in me that does not bear fruit he takes away, and every branch that does bear fruit he prunes, that it may bear more fruit. 3 Already you are clean because of the word that I have spoken to you. 4 Abide in me, and I in you. As the branch cannot bear fruit by itself, unless it abides in the vine, neither can you, unless you abide in me. 5 I am the vine; you are the branches. Whoever abides in me and I in him, he it is that bears much fruit, for apart from me you can do nothing. 6 If anyone does not abide in me he is thrown away like a branch and withers; and the branches are gathered, thrown into the fire, and burned. 7 If you abide in me, and my words abide in you, ask whatever you wish, and it will be done for you. 8 By this my Father is glorified, that you bear much fruit and so prove to be my disciples. 9 As the Father has loved me, so have I loved you. Abide in my love. 10 If you keep my commandments, you will abide in my love, just as I have kept my Father's commandments and abide in his love. 11 These things I have spoken to you, that my joy may be in you, and that your joy may be full.*

John 15: 1-11

ALTAR

²⁰ Then Noah built an altar to the L<small>ORD</small> and took some of every clean animal and some of every clean bird and offered burnt offerings on the altar. ²¹ And when the L<small>ORD</small> smelled the pleasing aroma, the L<small>ORD</small> said in his heart, "I will never again cursethe ground because of man, for the intention of man's heart is evil from his youth. Neither will I ever again strike down every living creature as I have done. ²² While the earth remains, seedtime and harvest, cold and heat, summer and winter, day and night, shall not cease."

Genesis 8: 20-22

Altars were built in Old Testament times to reflect significant occasions in the lives of God's people.

Noah built an altar when he landed on dry ground after being in the ark for five months. No doubt, Noah's motivation to build an altar and to offer burnt offerings on the same altar was motivated by extreme gratitude for the sparing of his entire family from the devastating flood. Additionally, atonement was always an integral aspect of burnt offerings.

¹⁰ But David's heart struck him after he had numbered the people. And David said to the L<small>ORD</small>, "I have sinned greatly in what I have done. But now, O L<small>ORD</small>, please take away the iniquity of your servant, for I have done very foolishly." ¹¹ And when David arose in the morning, the word of the L<small>ORD</small> came to the prophet Gad, David's seer, saying, ¹² "Go and say to David, 'Thus

says the LORD, Three things I offer you. Choose one of them, that I may do it to you.'" [13] So Gad came to David and told him, and said to him, "Shall three years of famine come to you in your land? Or will you flee three months before your foes while they pursue you? Or shall there be three days' pestilence in your land? Now consider, and decide what answer I shall return to him who sent me." [14] Then David said to Gad, "I am in great distress. Let us fall into the hand of the LORD, for his mercy is great; but let me not fall into the hand of man."

(It would benefit you if you read the remainder of the scripture from II Samuel 24: 10-25)

King David builds an altar after his ill motivated census drive. He sent out his key general Joab to conduct the census which counted only the men of fighting age. Joab questioned David because this was not the normal rationale for a census. However, Joab was obedient and the census revealed that David's army had 1,300,000 available troops. It is quite apparent that the sin in David's heart was one of pride. Perhaps his pride was similar to that of a wealthy farmer who rested in ease with his vast crops and built bigger barns to contain the excess.

David is now motivated to build an altar as an atonement for his sinful pride. He makes sure that the threshing floor is completely paid for before he makes it a site on which to construct the altar.

As an aside, did you note that David selected the three-day pestilence which resulted in 70,000 deaths before God put a stop to the angel that was causing the disease? The death rate almost is the same death rate that we as inhabitants of the USA are experiencing from our Covid-19 pandemic. Certainly, God is speaking to us. Are you listening?

We are beyond building altars. Maybe we need to set special symbols that become our own personal altars. When you reach those times in your life where you know that God is communicating with you through an illness, death of a family member, financial setback, marital problem etc. why not devise your own private altar. Perhaps such an altar might be a revised lifestyle, a financial revision toward God's kingdom, letting your friend know that you are concerned about him getting to know Jesus etc.

Prayer: Father, accept my prayer from an old hymn:

All to Jesus I surrender,

All to Him I freely give.

I will ever love and trust Him,

In His presence daily live.

All to Jesus I surrender,

Lord, I give myself to thee.

Fill me with Thy love and power,

Let Thy blessing fall on me. Amen

ASSURANCE

¹ Now faith is the assurance of things hoped for, the conviction of things not seen. ² For by it the people of old received their commendation. ³ By faith we understand that the universe was created by the word of God, so that what is seen was not made out of things that are visible.

Hebrews 11: 1-3

Assurance is not a vague hope but a full confidence that something in the future, not seen, but which has been promised by God, will come to pass. This confidence is based upon the biblical promise that if we place our faith in God who fully backs his promises because he is forever trustworthy. God has promised that he will never forsake his own.

A "soul mate" friend of mine posed the question as to "what is the origin of faith"? He thinks deeply and is very much "into the Word". The question cannot and should not be flippantly answered. I left the conversation without a definitive answer and it has been ruminating about in my mind for a rather long period of time.

Soon there will be another lunch with my very dear friend, and I have a more precise answer for him. My response will be something like the following brief explanation drawn from my own personal life's journey.

The story begins with a new location because of a career change. We were living in Traverse City and things were going nicely. We were in a friendly neighborhood and our church home was warm and biblically rock solid. (Our pastor was the late Warren Burgess) who was an absolute saint and just what we needed at this mid-point in our lives. Then everything changed.

Our family experienced six deaths over a two-year period. The last death was that of our oldest son, Mike. He never made it home from work one summer evening in August. A head – on traffic accident being the cause. Many years later the memories surrounding this point in our lives causes my very heart to clinch and for a tear to moisten my script.

So, faith for me has been and is best described as being on a continuum with hope at the left side and rock-solid assurance (faith) at the right. In between, there have been fluctuations based upon life's experiences and my perceptions of them.

Simply stated, faith in God ranges from wishy washy hope mixed with doubts to a rock-solid assurance of true faith in our creator, redeemer and source of our faith which rises and falls with the experiences of our lives.

What has worked in my life when I am overcome with doubts is that my prayers take on a greater depth. I also find solace especially in the Psalms. Psalm 30:5C states that: "weeping may tarry for the night, but joy comes with the morning."

So, at my next lunch with my friend, I'll give him a summation of this writing. Without a doubt, the topic will he discussed in detail and probably cause me to make minor corrections to my writing. However, the writing of Hebrews will be the source of our discussion.

The question on the table at the close of this writing is where are you regarding your assurance? Is it a weak hope or is it a solid faith? One thing is for sure, that God has allowed you to experience many peaks and valleys upon your journey toward eternity. It is my desire that you are solid in your assurance of faith.

Prayer: *Father, listen to your children praying at this moment. Move us toward the words of the hymn:*

Blessed Assurance

Blessed assurance, Jesus is mine!

Oh, what a foretaste of glory divine!

Heir of salvation, purchase of God,

Born of his Spirit, washed in his blood

Refrain

This is my story, this is my song,

Praising my Savior all the day long.

This is my story, this is my song,

Praising my Savior all the day long.

Amen

BE STILL

God is our refuge and strength,
a very present help in trouble.
2 Therefore we will not fear though the earth gives way,
though the mountains be moved into the heart of the
sea,
3 though its waters roar and foam,
though the mountains tremble at its swelling.
4 There is a river whose streams make glad the city of
God,
the holy habitation of the Most High.
5 God is in the midst of her; she shall not be moved;
God will help her when morning dawns.
6 The nations rage, the kingdoms totter;
he utters his voice, the earth melts.
7 The LORD of hosts is with us;
the God of Jacob is our fortress.
8 Come, behold the works of the LORD,
how he has brought desolations on the earth.
9 He makes wars cease to the end of the earth;
he breaks the bow and shatters the spear;
he burns the chariots with fire.
10 "Be still, and know that I am God.
I will be exalted among the nations,
I will be exalted in the earth!"
11 The LORD of hosts is with us;
the God of Jacob is our fortress.
Psalm 46

"Be still" is a phrase used by countless parents since the beginning of history. It can be used as an admonition or as words to soothe an upset infant being held in his mother's arms.

Christian bookstores have many decorative wall hangings that reflect the same words of comfort, "be still".

A correct biblical interpretation is that Psalm 46 is a hymn to celebrate Zion as a special place used by God as a focal point to bless the nations of the world. There are at least four other psalms with a similar message but Psalm 46 has the distinction of being widely used in Christian circles as a source of comfort. At the other end of the continuum of deep feelings is the word angst which expresses frustration   composed primarily of anxiety or dread.

Much of society deals with angst through avoidance in drugs and or alcohol. The alleviation of angst for unsettled feelings is only temporary and highly addictive.

In today's world there is almost zero time allocated to just being still. We are constantly bombarded by a cacophony of sounds, noise, solicited and non-solicited.

"Being still" then is basically a "time out" that we need to intentionally seek out. When we are in prayer it is absolutely the best time to just be still and take time to listen with our hearts as to what God wants us to hear.

"Being still" is enhanced by the rest of the phrase "and know that I am God" completes the promise. Knowing that God is always there for us. He not only "has our back" he also has our entire life. Does he have yours?

Prayer: Father my life sometimes causes me to become anxious with all the busyness and noise of everyday life. Give me a heart that finds rest in your promises of "Being Still and knowing that you are God". Amen

BE STRONG AND COURAGEOUS

Just as I was with Moses, so I will be with you. I will not leave you or forsake you. ⁶ *Be strong and courageous, for you shall cause this people to inherit the land that I swore to their fathers to give them.* ⁷ *Only be strong and very courageous, being careful to do according to all the law that Moses my servant commanded you. Do not turn from it to the right hand or to the left, that you may have good success[a] wherever you go.* ⁸ *This Book of the Law shall not depart from your mouth, but you shall meditate on it day and night, so that you may be careful to do according to all that is written in it. For then you will make your way prosperous, and then you will have good success.* ⁹ *Have I not commanded you? Be strong and courageous. Do not be frightened, and do not be dismayed, for the LORD your God is with you wherever you go."*

Joshua 1: 5b-9

At a Promise Keepers convention some years ago in Indianapolis, I heard a memorable sermon on being strong and courageous. It left an indelible impression upon me and colored my decision making in later years. God was speaking directly to Joshua just as he had spoken to Moses. God was basically saying to Joshua that "now you are in charge of the rest of the exodus, Be strong and courageous."

God of course knew what difficulties that Joshua would face in this singular leadership role. God used the same phrase to be strong and courageous three times. To repeat something three times in that culture was to give it maximum emphasis. God also promised Joshua success in his future venture of completing the exodus.

However, God's promise of success was tied to Joshua's obedience to the Book of the Law. This law extended at least through the Old Testament book of Deuteronomy. God was not promising financial wealth, but he was promising success in acquisition of the Promised Land.

"If Only" is a two-word phrase quite often expressed by people who when reminiscing about their past lives to rue decisions that they didn't make when in later analysis it appeared to be God's leading. So, if you are at a point of attempting to ascertain the leading of God, be strong and very courageous. God will bless your wise decision.

Prayer: Father, help me to be strong and very courageous. I wait for your leading in all my future decisions. Amen

BLESSING

24 The LORD bless you and keep you;
25 the LORD make his face to shine upon you and be gracious to you;
26 the LORD lift up his countenance upon you and give you peace.

Numbers 6: 24-26

This blessing which God gave to Moses who directed Aaron to bless the Israelites has been sung by choirs as a doxology. It is a beautiful piece of music and speaks to one's soul.

In some circles it is known as Aaron's Blessing or the Priestly Blessing. God blessed the Israelites by a successful exodus from Egypt to the promised land. In addition, they were blessed with good harvests, many offspring, peace and above all the presence of God. This presence was symbolized in the Ark of the Covenant, in the leading to the promised land by fire at night and a cloud by daylight.

Jesus spent the core of his Sermon on the Mount with emphasis on blessing as listed in the Beatitudes:

3 "Blessed are the poor in spirit, for theirs is the kingdom of heaven.
4 "Blessed are those who mourn, for they shall be comforted.
5 "Blessed are the meek, for they shall inherit the earth.
6 "Blessed are those who hunger and thirst for righteousness, for they shall be satisfied.

7 "Blessed are the merciful, for they shall receive mercy.
8 "Blessed are the pure in heart, for they shall see God.
9 "Blessed are the peacemakers, for they shall be called sons of God.
10 "Blessed are those who are persecuted for righteousness' sake, for theirs is the kingdom of heaven.
11 "Blessed are you when others revile you and persecute you and utter all kinds of evil against you falsely on my account. 12 Rejoice and be glad, for your reward is great in heaven, for so they persecuted the prophets who were before you.
Matthew 5: 3-12

The word blessing is used in modern day circles quite freely and often flippantly. However, the use of a blessing is often overlooked in everyday life. Why not let others know that they have been a blessing in your life? Also, when we approve of a new relationship, let the persons involved know that they have your blessing. Perhaps a bit old fashioned but often overlooked in today's society.

Let your spouse know that she is a blessing in your marriage. Her loving ways are often taken for granted. Your children need to hear that they are blessed. This will bring light and joy to those upon whom you render a blessing. What a way to let others know that we are Jesus' ambassadors.

Prayer: Father you have blessed us and perhaps we have taken your favor of blessing for granted. Now we just want to extend your blessing to others that need to hear from you. May it be done through us. Amen

Business Plan

13 Come now, you who say, "Today or tomorrow we will go into such and such a town and spend a year there and trade and make a profit"— 14 yet you do not know what tomorrow will bring. What is your life? For you are a mist that appears for a little time and then vanishes. 15 Instead you ought to say, "If the Lord wills, we will live and do this or that." 16 As it is, you boast in your arrogance. All such boasting is evil. 17 So whoever knows the right thing to do and fails to do it, for him it is sin.

James 4:13-17

What is your business plan is the key question asked by bankers and venture capitalists when an individual asks for a loan or for a line of credit?

However, no one knows for sure what the future will bring. We can't know for sure about our future because God has not revealed to us what the future will bring. Each person is one heartbeat away from eternity. So, is it wrong to plan for our futures? Or should we just live our lives without any sort of plan for the future?

Each one of us has cognitive skills that give us the ability to predict the future to the best of our mortal ability. Of course, we should then plan for the future to the best of our abilities. We will then submit our business plan after carefully looking at all the pros and cons that we can realistically predict what our future might hold.

However, the future is always the unforeseen such as a pandemic, recession, marriage failure, or accident that can drastically alter your plans.

Conversely, what are your plans for your immortal existence after you die? Each one of us will surely leave this life. Have you submitted your plan for life after death? You really can't put it off. None of us knows when we will cease to exist here on earth. We don't know what God has planned for us. Therefore, it is absolutely necessary for us to plan our immortal "business plan". Many of you have maybe planned for your last days in the form or a will and/or trust. Some have perhaps planned their funerals, and some have even prepaid for them. Others even have a burial plot reserved complete with a headstone. At death, your soul will leave your body and will reside in a destination of your selection. Have you made that eternal "business plan?"

Prayer: Father, I've always wanted to go to heaven when I die. I have not made the arrangements. Please forgive my sinful past and accept me into your present and eternal kingdom. Amen

CALLING

19 So he departed from there and found Elisha the son of Shaphat, who was plowing with twelve yoke of oxen in front of him, and he was with the twelfth. Elijah passed by him and cast his cloak upon him. 20 And he left the oxen and ran after Elijah and said, "Let me kiss my father and my mother, and then I will follow you." And he said to him, "Go back again, for what have I done to you?" 21 And he returned from following him and took the yoke of oxen and sacrificed them and boiled their flesh with the yokes of the oxen and gave it to the people, and they ate. Then he arose and went after Elijah and assisted him.

I Kings 19: 19-21

When I was a young boy about early elementary school age, I can recall my parents commenting about someone going into seminary because he had been "called". My assumption was that the individual had heard directly from God like Samuel when he was being mentored by Eli. Others such as Moses and Abraham also came to mind of ones who had been directly called to a special task.

Since those early years, I have come to the conclusion that pastors and others are called to serve in special ways but the calls are based upon interest, giftedness, and the urging and or mentoring of special people in their lives. These special people can be anyone who is close and respected by the one being called to a special task in the kingdom of God. Quite often the special people are schoolteachers, Sunday school teachers, youth ministers, parents, or a close friend.

Reflecting upon today's scripture, very few of us have been fortunate enough to be so closely mentored as was Elisha by Elijah. However, as we think back, many of us have had special people in our backgrounds that have affected our career choices.

The church that I attend has an excellent program that young people wishing to come forward and confess their faith before the congregation and God are plugged into a volunteer adult mentor who spends time with them, prays with them and explores in depth what it means to publicly claim Jesus as their Savior and Lord.

If you have come to the point in your life that you are a Christ follower, it is natural to further conclude that you are called. When one becomes a Christian, then it also means that one is called. Yes, we are indeed called to use our gifts, our time and our monies to further the kingdom. We are not called to just coast along waiting for our eternal reward. Just think of the many opportunities to serve. Just maybe those watching your life will be attracted to your life of service.

Prayer: Father, use me to be of service in whatever way I can. Take whatever you have given me and may I use it to further your kingdom. Amen

CHARIOTS

⁹ When they had crossed, Elijah said to Elisha, "Ask what I shall do for you, before I am taken from you." And Elisha said, "Please let there be a double portion of your spirit on me." ¹⁰ And he said, "You have asked a hard thing; yet, if you see me as I am being taken from you, it shall be so for you, but if you do not see me, it shall not be so." ¹¹ And as they still went on and talked, behold, chariots of fire and horses of fire separated the two of them. And Elijah went up by a whirlwind into heaven. ¹² And Elisha saw it and he cried, "My father, my father! The chariots of Israel and its horsemen!" And he saw him no more.
II Kings 2: 9-12

Chariots have always held a special place in my spiritual thinking. My cousin, Larry first made me aware of the significance of what he called the "great chariot ride" when he was referring to and anticipating his eternal reward. I've always imagined that his chariot was a special one because of the many souls he had introduced to the kingdom of heaven.

It all started our when Elijah was mentoring Elisha at the end of Elijah's life here on earth. At the end of their parting conversation, chariots of fire and horses of fire appeared, and Elijah was transported in a whirlwind directly into heaven. What a symbol of God's power and immediate blessing! Elisha is so overcome that he cries out, "My father, my father! The chariots of Israel and its horsemen!" Elisha has Elijah's cloak (mantel) which was a symbol of Elijah's power being transferred to Elisha. Elisha casts that same cloak upon the Jordan River and immediately the waters backed up and Elisha walked across the Jordan on a dry riverbed.

Someday each one of us will take a "great chariot ride." That ride will take place the moment of your last breath. Are you assured where your chariot is headed? In Philippians 1:22-24 it is clearly stated that a follower of Jesus will go directly to heaven.

Prayer:

Swing Low Sweet Chariot

Comin for to carry me home.

I'm sometimes up and sometimes down

Comin for to carry me home

But I know my soul is heaven bound

Comin for to carry me home.

Amen

CHILD DISCIPLINE

Whoever spares the rod hates his son,
but he who loves him is diligent to discipline him.

Proverbs 13:24

Child rearing today for the most part is far more physically gentle than in prior generations. Today spanking is most unusual and is viewed by many as child abuse. Instead, a "time out" is quite often the punishment for a youngster whose behavior needs adjustment.

In the Bible, the rod was often used as a means of discipline. The rod was a slim stick quite similar to a paint stirring stick of modern day.

Catholic schools quite often used a ruler to strike a student's hands when his behavior needed to be adjusted.

My generation (senior citizen) can remember that spanking was often used. A friend of mine had a leather strop used for honing straight edge razors upon which he had printed "I need thee every hour". The results of spanking were usually immediate in the form of tears and changed behavior.

Personally, when I was about seven years old, I announced to my mother that I was moving to my buddy Paul's house because their atmosphere was more to my liking. She even helped me pack by putting necessary items into a large red handkerchief which I knotted and inserted a sturdy stick, put it over my shoulder and proceeded to march to Paul's house. I had traveled for about 15 minutes when my older sister pulled alongside me on her bike. Her words turned me around immediately because when she said that mom was frying chicken for supper and that was my favorite meal. I was greeted by my mom who had the green shoots from a fig tree stump in her hand. These were applied to my backside with her muttering words sounding like "never again". The welts subsided; the words remained permanently etched in my little boy's heart. After that session, Paul's house is by special invitation and approved by both moms.

My senior citizen ideas of child rearing are not to attempt to tell others on how to raise their children. Every home has their own methods. My singular input is to not overdo a particular method. If you occasionally spank, do so out of love and not your own personal anger. Non conditional love needs to be the theme of child rearing. Our heavenly father has so loved us without condition and purely out of grace.

Prayer: Father give me a cool head as I discipline my children. May my behavior reflect how you have and are loving me with pure grace. Amen

CONTENTMENT

He who loves money will not be satisfied with money,
nor he who loves wealth with his income.
Ecclesiastes 5:10
No one can serve two masters, for either he will hate
the one and love the other, or he will be devoted to the
one and despise the other. You cannot serve God and
money.
Matthew 6:24
But those who desire to be rich fall into temptation,
into a snare, into many senseless and harmful desires
that plunge people into ruin and destruction.10 For the
love of money is the root of all kinds of evils. It is
through this craving that some have wandered away
from the faith and pierced themselves with many
pangs.
I Timothy 6:9-10
Keep your life free from the love of money, and be
content with what you have, for he has said, "I will
never leave you nor forsake you."
Hebrews 13:5

Money has been a key factor in the futuristic thinking efforts in the city in which I live. Philanthropy by wealthy individuals has developed medicine, the arts and general business climate to a point of enviable excellence.

For contentment to exist, the love of money cannot be present. So what is the difference between the love of money and contentment? There is no magical formula or equation that can answer the question "how much is enough?"

Those with great wealth that are actively blessing civic endeavors, Christian causes, and funding efforts to be obedient to the Great Commission are examples of money stewardship and will be able to "go through the eye of a needle" into their eternal reward. Money has not been their love. The kingdom of God has been their passion and consequently their one source of contentment.

To those who seriously question what constitutes the love of money should analyze their level of giving to causes of God's kingdom by setting up a simple balance sheet with two columns.

Net Worth   Kingdom Donations

The result of your analysis will probably be like our response when we are asked similar questions at the great judgment.

Parting light thought; it is not a sin to have adequate resources to fund possible assisted living and/or nursing home care. However, it's not necessary to set aside enough assets to buy the institution.

Go with God and do not let greed shadow your contentment.

Prayer: Father you are my "All in All". Give me contentment with your assets that you have given to me temporarily to increase your kingdom. Amen

CUP

5 The LORD is my chosen portion and my cup;
you hold my lot.
6 The lines have fallen for me in pleasant places;
indeed, I have a beautiful inheritance.
Psalm 16: 5-6

When one refers to their cup it can literally mean their portion. The psalmist, David spoke to his personal satisfaction with God's portion or cup that he had been given in life. In today's society it is quite unusual for people to express their comfort in God's providential care. Instead, we are surrounded by a general clamor of individuals that want more and more. We seldom hear expressions of thankful people who are living a life of gratitude.

Going on, each one of us has been given a cup. That is, we are at a place in our lives that we have many available options as to what to do with the cup of blessing given to us by God. Simple acts such as showing love to a child as stated in Matthew 23:25,26. Yes just a cup of cold water is an act of love.

- Woe to you, scribes and Pharisees, hypocrites! For you clean the outside of the cup and the plate, but inside they are full of greed and self-indulgence.
- You blind Pharisee! First clean the inside of the cup and the plate, that the outside may also be clean.

In Matthew 23 Jesus takes the scribes and Pharisees to task in that he exposes the phony religious acts as shallow and specifically designed to gain the applause of others. Again, the subject of a cup comes up but in a totally different manner. When David was grateful for his cup or portion it was a symbol of God's blessing upon his life. By contrast, when Jesus spoke of a cup in relation to the scribes and Pharisees, the cup was pointed out as a symbol of hypocrisy. Jesus said that you clean the outside of the cup until it gleams. Others by observation will only see the outside of the beautiful cup but inside it is full of greed and self-indulgence.

You and I have been given a portion of blessings which is symbolized as our "cup". Are you thanking God for your portion as David? Or are you just showing a shiny exterior? Take just a moment of silence and look inward. How is your cup?

Prayer: Father, thank you for my cup of blessing. Today I will look more carefully at the inside of my cup and take an effort to clean up my cup so that all can see you through me. Amen

CURTAIN

51 And behold, the curtain of the temple was torn in two, from top to bottom. And the earth shook, and the rocks were split. 52 The tombs also were opened. And many bodies of the saints who had fallen asleep were raised, 53 and coming out of the tombs after his resurrection they went into the holy city and appeared to many. 54 When the centurion and those who were with him, keeping watch over Jesus, saw the earthquake and what took place, they were filled with awe and said, "Truly this was the Son of God!"

Matthew 27: 51-54

Curtains in our lives are decorative and are meant to be pleasing and complimentary additions to the décor of the room. By contrast, the Temple of Herod, which was in existence during the time of Jesus, featured a massive curtain which separated the Holy Place from the Most Holy Place. This curtain was 62 feet high and 30 feet wide. It was elaborately woven of 72 plaits which consisted of twisted 24 threads each. The high priest could only enter the Most Holy Place once per year to sprinkle incense and blood to atone for the sins of the people.

This curtain was torn in two during Jesus crucifixion. Its significance symbolized the separation between God and his people was now nonexistent. The power of the crucifixion was further symbolized by splitting rocks and saints rising from their graves. Regular earthquakes do not split rocks, open graves, resurrect deceased bodies, and split heavy intricately woven fabric. No wonder the centurion and those with him who were guarding the crucifixion were moved to exclaim. "truly this was the Son of God!"

19 Therefore, brothers, since we have confidence to enter the holy places by the blood of Jesus, 20 by the new and living way that he opened for us through the curtain, that is, through his flesh, 21 and since we have a great priest over the house of God, 22 let us draw near with a true heart in full assurance of faith, with our hearts sprinkled clean from an evil conscience and our bodies washed with pure water. 23 Let us hold fast the confession of our hope without wavering, for he who promised is faithful. 24 And let us consider how to stir up one another to love and good works, 25 not neglecting to meet together, as is the habit of some, but encouraging one another, and all the more as you see the Day drawing near.

Hebrews 10:19-25

Perhaps some of us have doubts about the crucifixion of Jesus. Some questions which might be asked are "did the crucifixion really take away my sin?" The excerpt from Hebrews answers the question about the power of the crucifixion. The temple curtain was torn in two and the symbolism of that tearing of cloth gives us confidence to enter the Most Holy Place. Yes, there are no more dividers. We have direct access to the throne of God through the power of prayer. Our sins have been accounted for on the cross of Jesus. There is nothing that stands in the way of our adoration and praise.

This is a mind-blowing part of our salvation. No more barriers. No curtain. Just you and God. Let's go to him now in prayer.

Prayer: Father, thank you for making my sins be accounted for by the power of the crucifixion. I am in awe. I worship you and want to make every day a day of thankful living. Amen

DEMOCRACY

Every four years, America has a presidential election, every six years for senators and every two years for representatives. We have a voice in the choosing of key leadership positions for those individuals that set policy, law and budget for the governing of America. As a Christian, are we expected to select who we vote for based upon where each individual stands according to biblical standards? It is my opinion and supported by scripture that we are responsible for making our selection known at the ballot box that is consistent with where each individual stands in respect to Christian standards. If we don't exercise the right of Christian selection, then who will?

As a Christian we should have a mental filter which judges candidates based upon where they stand on key issues such as the following:

Their Relationship with Jesus

Abortion

Economy

Supreme Court Nominees

Climate Change

Definition of Marriage

Sexual Preference

Constitutional Stance

Personal Life

Trade

Military Strength

Health Care

Negotiation Skills

Our present president has a motto title "Make America Great Again". Think about that message. Many in our educational institutions are in the process of getting the message across that America was never great but was founded on religious bigotry and endorsement of slavery. When one is sheltered by the First Amendment right of free speech and institutional tenure the educators have a "bully pulpit" that can only be controlled by management that is conservative and Christian. The natural outcome of this liberal propaganda is a millennial push for socialism. These young minds have no idea where the monies will come from to finance their utopian dreams.

Parents, you are urged to make every effort to make sure that your college bound family members take a long look at how history is taught, what the sociology department is advocating and what the philosophy department is saying about absolute truth in the college that you are considering.

Prayer: Father, some of us have hidden our votes from others because we have voted for candidates that meet our standards of being glib and having a polished demeanor but who are not holding views that are consistent with biblical mandates. Please forgive our past sins of endorsing non-Christian views. We will vote in a Christ like manner in the future.

We ask you to continue to bless America and our efforts to be consistent in our Christian walk. Amen

DORCAS

36 Now there was in Joppa a disciple named Tabitha, which, translated, means Dorcas. She was full of good works and acts of charity. 37 In those days she became ill and died, and when they had washed her, they laid her in an upper room. 38 Since Lydda was near Joppa, the disciples, hearing that Peter was there, sent two men to him, urging him, "Please come to us without delay." 39 So Peter rose and went with them. And when he arrived, they took him to the upper room. All the widows stood beside him weeping and showing tunics and other garments that Dorcas made while she was with them. 40 But Peter put them all outside, and knelt down and prayed; and turning to the body he said, "Tabitha, arise." And she opened her eyes, and when she saw Peter she sat up. 41 And he gave her his hand and raised her up. Then, calling the saints and widows, he presented her alive. 42 And it became known throughout all Joppa, and many believed in the Lord.

Acts 9: 36-42

My mother was like Dorcas, full of good works. She worked as a dietician in the local hospital from the early 1940's until the mid 1970's. She freely donated her time and available monies to her church. At her retirement and later at her funeral she was recognized for her selfless attitude and wonderful fruit pies. At both functions she was affectionately referred to as "Sweetie Pie".

In today's scripture passage we see Peter being summoned to the seacoast city of Joppa to attend to the recently deceased Dorcas. Her weeping friends were admiring her creative sewing efforts of tunics and other garments. Peter shooed the widows out of the room and through the power of God via Peter's prayer, life was restored back to Dorcas. We don't know what happened to Dorcas after her resurrection, but we can imagine that her ministry of good works and charity was not only accelerated but also salted with her story of the healing power of God.

Why the resurrection of Dorcas? Just before Dorcas was resurrected, Peter had previously healed the paralyzed Aeneas. Now that the people were paying closer attention to the gospel through the healings that had taken place, the stage of public opinion and attention was ready for the gospel to be introduced to also include the Gentiles. Peter is made aware of the timing for the addition of the Gentiles in a vision that showed him that the Old Testament forbidden foods are now approved. The lesson for Peter is now the gospel is available for all peoples regardless of their backgrounds.

Back to Dorcas. There is no such thing as a person who comes to salvation by only living a life of obedience. Yes, our good works are the way of living a thankful life but in addition, we need to give our hearts to accept the plan of salvation through Jesus' death upon the cross. Hebrews 12:1 says that we are surrounded by a great cloud of witnesses. What are they seeing in your life?" Are they seeing not only good works but the good works of a redeemed life?

Prayer: Father, may my life show that you are my "All in All" in works and in speech. Amen

DOUBTS

29 He said, "Come." So Peter got out of the boat and walked on the water and came to Jesus. 30 But when he saw the wind,[a] he was afraid, and beginning to sink he cried out, "Lord, save me."

Matthew 14:29-30

While having coffee with a close friend, the topic of doubting came up. We both confessed that that at times we experienced doubts. My memorable doubts have come at a time when my world came crashing down. A phone call, an accident, my oldest son had died at the scene. Only 23 years old, a new father, a budding position as a chemist, a new homeowner. Why!!! How could God allow this to happen to our family of devout Christians? Doubts overwhelmed me. The depressive doubts gradually faded into an elevation of spirit.

Various factors helped elevate my spirit. I spent many hours in meditation and prayer. Cell phones were not on the scene, so my hours spent in thought and meditation were truly serene in my fishing boat trying to catch muskies on a small Traverse City area lake. The muskies were evasive, but healing was beginning.

Friends who had also experienced the loss of a child became a small group of support. It amazed me that so many couples had experienced a similar loss. Work associates and clients had all heard the news and my depressive thoughts grew smaller with my successive telling the story of how and when the accident took place.

Life's trials such as job loss, financial setback and marital stress are just a few of life's problems that trigger doubts. The real question is how are you handling the doubts? A common response is to bury the doubt and put on a brave facade. Such an approach might hide the depressive doubt from our friends, but we know that God knows all about our doubts and depression.

So, if God knows and yet even allows us to wallow in our quagmire of doubts, where are you at with your relationship with God? I have friends that are holding a grudge against God for allowing sad things to happen within their lives. How do I influence them to be open and to deal with their internal hate of God? Frankly, this situation stumps me and perhaps there is not a magical solution except to be a positive influence and to live in an open fashion with my God.

Being a soul-mate is one with whom you can share the deepest concerns of your life and never have to be concerned with others finding out because a true soul-mate listens to you, prays with and for you and always "has your back".

So why did Jesus curse the fig tree? The fig tree was the picture of health with abundant green leaves but was not bearing figs. The quick answer is that Jesus was using the fig tree as an illustration for the disciples.

Our doubts are spoken to when Jesus compares our faith to an abundant crop of figs. With faith our lives bear the scrutiny of others. The abundance of fruit is observed in our acts of love and care for others.

Prayer: Father as others see me may they also see you in my fruit filled life. Amen

ETERNITY

Truly, truly, I say to you, whoever hears my word and believes him who sent me has eternal life. He does not come into judgement but has passed from death to life. John 5:24

I write these things to you who believe in the name of the Son of God, that you may know that you have eternal life. I John 5:13

[9] What gain has the worker from his toil? [10] I have seen the business that God has given to the children of man to be busy with. [11] He has made everything beautiful in its time. Also, he has put eternity into man's heart, yet so that he cannot find out what God has done from the beginning to the end. [12] I perceived that there is nothing better for them than to be joyful and to do good as long as they live; [13] also that everyone should eat and drink and take pleasure in all his toil—this is God's gift to man.

Ecclesiastes 3:9-13

Eternity is a topic that man can't begin to describe because as man understands the concept of time there is a beginning and an end. However, eternity as depicted in the Bible is without beginning or end. Consequently, we are now involved in eternity. The eternity of one who hears the gospel and believes is presently in process!

The second scripture found in I John goes a step further. It plainly says that you who believe in the name of the Son of God will know that you now have eternal life. Yes, now here on earth, you are experiencing the beginning of eternal life. At death, our souls will join others who have gone on before us to the glorious extension of our eternity. When one goes back to examine the original Greek language the word eternal not only indicates length to life but also quality. Right now, as a believer you are experiencing the initial quality of eternity that will be in glory beyond description and will have no end!

One of the more vibrant churches that I'm somewhat familiar with recently went through an in-depth analysis of their ministry. The evaluator looked at all the facets of ministry including preaching education, parking, security, attendance gains and losses etc. were just some of the points covered in the evaluation.   A particular issue raised by the analysis pointed out that the church as a whole is convinced that eternal life in heaven was where they were heading at death. However, they did not appear to be living a joyful life here on earth.

The writer of Ecclesiastes (probably Solomon) said virtually the same thing as the church evaluator pointed out. The scripture says that you live in a beautiful creation and God has put eternity within your hearts. Therefore, enjoy the part of eternity that you are now experiencing and celebrate. Enjoy this day! It is the day the Lord has made! Psalm 118:24

Prayer: Father, we have failed to celebrate the beginning of our eternity in our present time on earth. May we take special efforts to live a joyful life that others may see you living within us. Amen

FACE TO FACE

[17] And the LORD said to Moses, "This very thing that you have spoken I will do, for you have found favor in my sight, and I know you by name." [18] Moses said, "Please show me your glory." [19] And he said, "I will make all my goodness pass before you and will proclaim before you my name 'The LORD.' And I will be gracious to whom I will be gracious, and will show mercy on whom I will show mercy. [20] But," he said, "you cannot see my face, for man shall not see me and live." [21] And the LORD said, "Behold, there is a place by me where you shall stand on the rock, [22] and while my glory passes by I will put you in a cleft of the rock, and I will cover you with my hand until I have passed by. [23] Then I will take away my hand, and you shall see my back, but my face shall not be seen."

Exodus 33: 17-23

Face masks are presently mandatory in all business places by both staff and customers. In fact, when outdoors, masks are necessary when social distancing is not possible. These measures are mandated in the state of Michigan by the governor in an attempt to lower the exposure to the pandemic Covid-19. There is an element of political and public health driving the governor's decision.

Moses was attempting to see God face to face. However, Moses was to see God through the many episodes of mercy that God had shown before and during the exodus. God made his presence known by fire

48

at night and by a cloud during the day. Another outstanding illustration of God's mercy was in the parting of the Red Sea allowing for safe passage to the far shore. The release of the dammed-up waters drowning their Egyptian army and their 600 chariots was another illustration of God's mercy.

Today, we are surrounded by the mercies of God. Many of these mercies have been experienced by those reading this meditation. The healings from major illnesses, the recovery from financial distress, the close calls in our automobiles etc. The question for each one of us who have been shown the mercies of God is "did it make a difference in your relationship with God?" We are presently in the figurative "boot camp" of our earthly existence. Are you sensitive to the many mercies of our heavenly father?

We have been prepared for witnessing the majesty of God. No more masks, no more mercies, only majesty. A majesty that we cannot possibly comprehend. We shall see our Father God face to face.

Instead of a traditional prayer, let's close this meditation with the blessing given by Moses to Aaron shortly before Aaron's advent into seeing the majesty of God face to face in glory.

The Lord bless you and keep you;

The Lord make his face to shine upon you and be gracious to you;

The Lord lift up his countenance upon you and give you peace. Amen

FEAR

My wife commented from time to time that today's generation doesn't fear God. Her meaning was that they lack a reverence and an awe of God. More precisely, a deeper meaning is that over the years there has been an erosion of how God is perceived. A former generation pictured God as a god of absolutes. He was envisioned as a holy God that loved those created in his image and held them accountable for where they placed their love and devotion. One weakness of that former generation is that they did not place enough emphasis on the loving attribute of God.

In modern thinking, the phrase "my god wouldn't do that" reflects a change in perception of how God is perceived. One can envision each person with an internal balance scale of weighing how we perceive God to fit into our comfort zone. This is amazingly similar to cultures of the past who carved their perception of God utilizing stone and/or wood into idols. Our only change of today is that we have not crafted God into an idol but instead our idols are what we bow down to with our time and money. Perhaps we will put god into our technology of a God app on our cellphones.

If our conception of God is to our imagination and liking and is not a God of absolutes as in the Bible, then when we are faced with the things of life that cause us to fear such as job loss, marital instability, financial loss, death of a loved one etc. then how do you want your God to respond? I suspect that the God of your making is not capable and available.

The following verses from Hebrews states who the real God is and ever shall be:

13 For when God made a promise to Abraham, since he had no one greater by whom to swear, he swore by himself, 14 saying, "Surely I will bless you and multiply you." 15 And thus Abraham,[a] having patiently waited, obtained the promise. 16 For people swear by something greater than themselves, and in all their disputes an oath is final for confirmation. 17 So when God desired to show more convincingly to the heirs of the promise the unchangeable character of his purpose, he guaranteed it with an oath, 18 so that by two unchangeable things, in which it is impossible for God to lie, we who have fled for refuge might have strong encouragement to hold fast to the hope set before us. 19 We have this as a sure and steadfast anchor of the soul, a hope that enters into the inner place behind the curtain,

Hebrews 6:13-19

Prayer: Father, the words of II Timothy 1:7 is our closing prayer: For God gave us a spirit not of fear but of power and love and self-control. Amen

FOCUS

19 He entered Jericho and was passing through. 2 And behold, there was a man named Zacchaeus. He was a chief tax collector and was rich. 3 And he was seeking to see who Jesus was, but on account of the crowd he could not, because he was small in stature. 4 So he ran on ahead and climbed up into a sycamore tree to see him, for he was about to pass that way. 5 And when Jesus came to the place, he looked up and said to him, "Zacchaeus, hurry and come down, for I must stay at your house today." 6 So he hurried and came down and received him joyfully. 7 And when they saw it, they all grumbled, "He has gone in to be the guest of a man who is a sinner." 8 And Zacchaeus stood and said to the Lord, "Behold, Lord, the half of my goods I give to the poor. And if I have defrauded anyone of anything, I restore it fourfold." 9 And Jesus said to him, "Today salvation has come to this house, since he also is a son of Abraham. 10 For the Son of Man came to seek and to save the lost."

Luke 19: 1-10

An excellent football program on a college level is gaining national attention because of their focus. They have adopted an accelerated program of weight conditioning and additional emphasis on more speed. The program is beginning to be noticed on the playing field especially during the fourth quarter where their enhanced conditioning begins to be observed.

Zacchaeus was an example of intense focus in that he made sure that he would be able to see Jesus when he came by. Little did he realize that Jesus not only spotted him, but Jesus also saw into his heart before he had a conversation with him. What a wonderful night was in store for Zacchaeus, a dinner with much conversation and Jesus as a house guest!

A lesson can be learned from Zacchaeus in that he made every effort to make sure that he saw Jesus. Are we that intense in our efforts to see Jesus? We have so many opportunities to see Jesus in the form of Sunday worship, Christian education in the form of Bible studies and Sunday School classes. How about doing some volunteer work for a downtown mission? What Christian book have you recently read? How about a Christian movie? In addition, there are mission trips that might need your presence and/or funding. The list of possibilities is almost endless.

Perhaps, as you read this short meditation, a thought comes to mind of something you could do or become involved in. Maybe it might be the inner working of the Holy Spirit trying to get your attention. Perhaps it might be an opportunity for you to become more focused in your quest to better see Jesus.

Prayer: Father, forgive my past cavalier attitude of just doing what was expected of me for your kingdom instead of becoming more intensely focused on you and your kingdom. Amen

GOD OF ALL COMFORT

3 Blessed be the God and Father of our Lord Jesus Christ, the Father of mercies and God of all comfort. 4 Who comforts us in all our affliction, so that we may be able to comfort those who are in any affliction, with the comfort with which we ourselves are comforted by God. 5 For as we share abundantly in Christ's sufferings, so through Christ we share abundantly in comfort too. 6 If we are afflicted, it is for your comfort and salvation; and if we are comforted, it is for your comfort, which you experience when you patiently endure the same sufferings that we suffer. Our hope for you is unshaken, for we know that as you share in our sufferings, you will also share in our comfort.
II Corinthians 1: 3-7

The apostle Paul relates that he had experienced great troubles. Apparently, the church at Corinth was familiar with Paul's recent problems in that they are not described. We are however led to believe that the problems which Paul experienced were so intense that they were life threatening.

Paul gives thanks to God from whom he had received comfort after his afflictions. It is this model that of receiving comfort that we can pass on comfort to others.

Our family received such comfort when our son entered glory as the result of a car accident. Other parents who had experienced the loss of a child were there for us and their presence and words were of great comfort to us.

We can reflect God's comfort to others especially when we have walked down a similar path. When attempting to comfort others that are hurting, the main factor to consider is to be genuine. Never attempt to offer trite platitudes such a "I know how you feel" when in fact you have not personally experienced similar problems.

When you are at a loss for words to extend comfort, just let the hurting persons know that they are loved and prayed for.

We typically grow more as Christ followers when we are in the middle of a difficult period in our life. This is a time to spend deeper time in the Word and in prayer. Jesus will be there for you. He has your heart!

Prayer: Father give me a heart for others that need comfort. Amen

10 And he called the people to him and said to them, "Hear and understand: 11 it is not what goes into the mouth that defiles a person, but what comes out of the mouth; this defiles a person." 12 Then the disciples came and said to him, "Do you know that the Pharisees were offended when they heard this saying?" 13 He answered, "Every plant that my heavenly Father has not planted will be rooted up. 14 Let them alone; they are blind guides.[a] And if the blind lead the blind, both will fall into a pit." 15 But Peter said to him, "Explain the parable to us." 16 And he said, "Are you also still without understanding? 17 Do you not see that whatever goes into the mouth passes into the stomach and is expelled?[b] 18 But what comes out of the mouth proceeds from the heart, and this defiles a person. 19 For out of the heart come evil thoughts, murder, adultery, sexual immorality, theft, false witness, slander. 20 These are what defile a person. But to eat with unwashed hands does not defile anyone."

Matthew 15: 10-20

Today, heart disease is one of the leading causes of death in the USA. We are a nation that is basically number one globally in our standard of living. We can eat almost anything because we can afford it. Eating an unhealthy amount and type of food and lack of exercise appear to be the main contributing factors to heart disease.

What about our spiritual hearts? What defiles a person's heart? Our scripture of today explains very completely that it is out of our hearts that come all of our words and actions. Our thoughts lead us to action and speaking. So where is your heart? If you have impure thoughts, what have you done about it? Have you acted out those thoughts and asked for forgiveness or are you living a life that is motivated by impure thoughts and you have concluded that you might as well go on living without moral restrictions because you just can't be forgiven?

Jesus has the answer for you. He and he alone can forgive all your impure thoughts and actions. Just ask him to take over your heart and he will forgive all of your sins of the past, present and future. Once your give yourself over to Jesus, all of your past is over. No more regrets and feelings of guilt. Jesus died on the cross and arose from the dead to conquer sin for everyone who gives their heart over to him. So friend, where are you at? Where's your heart? Jesus is knocking at the door of your life. Do you hear him?

Prayer: Jesus, you paid the price for all of the sins in the world. Please accept my plea for your mercy and forgiveness. I want to serve you from now on.   Amen

HOPE

18 For I consider that the sufferings of this present time are not worth comparing with the glory that is to be revealed to us. 19 For the creation waits with eager longing for the revealing of the sons of God. 20 For the creation was subjected to futility, not willingly, but because of him who subjected it, in hope 21 that the creation itself will be set free from its bondage to corruption and obtain the freedom of the glory of the children of God. 22 For we know that the whole creation has been groaning together in the pains of childbirth until now. 23 And not only the creation, but we ourselves, who have the first fruits of the Spirit, groan inwardly as we wait eagerly for adoption as sons, the redemption of our bodies. 24 For in this hope we were saved. Now hope that is seen is not hope. For who hopes for what he sees? 25 But if we hope for what we do not see, we wait for it with patience.
Romans 8:18-25

Wherever you are at right now, do you have hope? More clearly, are you waiting for a time when your situation will be improved?

Many of us hope for a variety of things and/or situations. Some are waiting to get married or to have our situation change so that marriage is more predictable. Others are waiting for family dynamics to change so that relationships can improve. Others are hoping for a job or for a better job. We need more money, and our working conditions are very unenjoyable to say the least.

Most of our hoping is for positive results that we can already predict and visualize. So our hope is possibly coveting what is sinful and unattainable. This level of hoping is more like wishful thinking in that we hope for goals that are beyond our physical realm because we are limited by money concerns or we are hoping for something sinful.

The hope referred to in today's scripture is on a totally different level. We can't see or imagine the hope that is being sought after. It is our ultimate hope of what will be our role in the second resurrection. Christ will physically return; bodies will come out of their graves. These bodies will be restored in a glorified form. This is our ultimate hope. This hope can't be described because if we knew exactly the details of the second resurrection it wouldn't truly be hope in its purest form.

Where are you at? Do you hope for Jesus to return or does that thought cause you great fear? Are your fears based upon doubts that you don't know for sure where your eternal home will be? You can be sure if you give over your life to Jesus as you savior. You can pray right now for Jesus to forgive all your past and present sins. When you have made that request, then promise to turn your life around and serve Jesus in your thoughts, actions and words. In so doing you now have more than just hope. You have assurance. You have faith. Welcome home!   Amen

HOW THEN SHOULD WE LIVE

*¹³ Therefore, preparing your minds for action,
and being sober-minded, set your hope fully on the
grace that will be brought to you at the revelation
of Jesus Christ.
¹⁴ As obedient children, do not be conformed to the
passions of your former ignorance,
¹⁵ but as he who called you is holy, you also be holy in
all your conduct,
¹⁶ since it is written, "You shall be holy, for I am holy."
¹⁷ And if you call on him as Father
who judges impartially.
according to each one's deeds, conduct yourselves with
fear throughout the time of your exile,
I Peter 1: 13-17*

As of this writing, it is about one month before the most contentious presidential election in recent history. (2020) America is deeply divided. Rioting, burning of property and looting are taking place in some of our major cities without administrative efforts to quell the destruction. Federal help has been offered but some mayors have denied the use of the National Guard to restore order. So chaos is being allowed and endorsed. The police departments in some cities have been reduced in number and their jobs are being redefined so that their efforts are to become more like social workers than officers that use force when necessary to bring compliance.

There is such dissension on the part of political parties, that one cannot have a political discussion involving persons that have allegiance to differing political parties. At this time we are called to be holy by the above scripture. That is a challenge!

Families are also sharply divided. The millennial generation tends toward liberal policies whereas older family members typically are where the conservatives are found. The tension is so great that political discussions within the family are exceedingly difficult.

Concurrent with this divisive political thinking, there is a pandemic called Covid-19 which the will probably not be stopped until a vaccine is available. Presently, such a vaccine appears to be available during the coming winter months.

So how do we conduct ourselves during this contentious time? Be holy? That's the short answer but how does one live a life of holiness?

The hard answer to how to be holy is to listen before offering solutions and opinions. Read up on the differences so that we can be at peace with our own assumptions. Change ourselves if we are not taking a Christian stand. Vote as a Christian! Do not try to change the opinions of those that differ from your opinion.

Prayer: Father forgive my need to be vocal and controlling because I know that I'm right. Instead, in my quest for greater holiness, soften my heart, give me a loving ear and may my actions toward holiness be the unspoken words that lead others closer to you. Amen

"I CAN'T HEAR YOU"

¹⁴ Indeed, in their case the prophecy of Isaiah is
fulfilled that says:

""'"You will indeed hear but never understand,
and you will indeed see but never perceive."
¹⁵ For this people's heart has grown dull,
and with their ears they can barely hear,
and their eyes they have closed,
lest they should see with their eyes
and hear with their ears
and understand with their heart
and turn, and I would heal them.'

¹⁶ But blessed are your eyes, for they see, and your
ears, for they hear.

Matthew 13:14-16

We hear God through reading his word. In addition, we
hear God through bible-based preaching. Sometimes,
we hear God through the words and/or actions of
others.

Within each of us is an inner voice that speaks to our
inner self (our soul). This is a vital aspect to hearing. We
can hear but not really internalize what is being said.
Another way of hearing is to really pay attention and
then to respond positively in words or actions to the
spiritual advice or information.

Many of us hear but we don't obey. Instead, we go our
own way and pretend that what we are doing is okay,

but we really know better. An illustration that follows came from a conversation I recently had with a friend.

This friend was wading in the lake in front of his summer home and noticed his two-year-old grandson, Christopher, walking on the neighbor's dock and not wearing the required life jacket which was in direct violation of grandpa and grandma's rule that youngsters up to a certain age must wear life jackets when walking on the docks. Grandpa immediately called "Christopher you need to put on a life jacket". Christopher didn't even look toward his grandpa but kept on walking. Grandpa again called out "Christopher" in an outdoor voice. (retired educators do not lose volume with age). Christopher continued his own way and grandpa yelled "Christopher stop and get on a life jacket!" Christopher never looked at grandpa but responded with great clarity" grandpa, I can't hear you!"

Today, as you walk along on the dock of the journey of your life, do you have on your life jacket? Simply stated, do you know for sure that heaven is your destination? If you have any doubt, Jesus will welcome you with open arms regardless of your past non hearing behavior. It's time to listen, to hear and to ask Jesus into your life.

Prayer: Father some of us are going through the motions but we need assurance. Give us that faith as we come to your invitation with hearing ears and loving hearts. Amen

JOSEPH AND NICODEMUS

31 Since it was the day of Preparation, and so that the bodies would not remain on the cross on the Sabbath (for that Sabbath was a high day), the Jews asked Pilate that their legs might be broken and that they might be taken away. 32 So the soldiers came and broke the legs of the first, and of the other who had been crucified with him. 33 But when they came to Jesus and saw that he was already dead, they did not break his legs. 34 But one of the soldiers pierced his side with a spear, and at once there came out blood and water. 35 He who saw it has borne witness—his testimony is true, and he knows that he is telling the truth—that you also may believe. 36 For these things took place that the Scripture might be fulfilled: "Not one of his bones will be broken." 37 And again another Scripture says, "They will look on him whom they have pierced."

38 After these things Joseph of Arimathea, who was a disciple of Jesus, but secretly for fear of the Jews, asked Pilate that he might take away the body of Jesus, and Pilate gave him permission. So he came and took away his body. 39 Nicodemus also, who earlier had come to Jesus by night, came bringing a mixture of myrrh and aloes, about seventy-five pounds in weight. 40 So they took the body of Jesus and bound it in linen cloths with the spices, as is the burial custom of the Jews. 41 Now in the place where he was crucified there was a garden, and in the garden a new tomb in which no one had yet been laid. 42 So because of the Jewish day of Preparation, since the tomb was close at hand, they laid Jesus there.

John 19:31-42

If I were the executor of Jesus' estate, I would have asked the disciples to take care of Jesus' body and find an appropriate burial location. After all, these eleven men had been with Jesus for three years of preaching, healing and conversing with one another. It would be only appropriate for the disciples to take proper final care of their best friend and Savior.

However, God had a precise plan all worked out as to the final arrangements. Joseph of Arimathea, a member of the Jewish Council, the Sanhedrin, was a secret believer in Jesus. Politically, he could not go public with his faith. However, because of his position in the Sanhedrin, he gains an audience with Pilate and asks for Jesus' body. Pilate readily agrees because of the Day of Preparation and the upcoming Sabbath, the body needed to be removed. This quick disposition of the body of Jesus would meet all the religious requirements of Jewish religious traditions.

From out of nowhere, Nicodemus shows up on the scene. He also is a secret believer. He can't go public because he is a Pharisee. Nicodemus is loaded down with seventy-five pounds of expensive burial spices consisting of aloe and myrrh plus linen cloths in which to wrap the body.

Notice the unheralded burial scene of two converted underground Christians being given the distinct honor of burying the Savior of the World! Can't you just imagine their conversation? Getting acquainted and discovering that they shared the same plan of salvation. Through their tears of grief there were also tears of joy that two members of the daytime "in crowd" could have the honor of burying their Savior.

As an aside, this tomb belonged to Joseph of Arimathea. It was brand new. It had been cut from raw rock and was an elegant tomb. In fact the stone which was used to cover the entrance to the tomb was also cut by stone masons. It was a perfect circle measuring 4.5 ft. in diameter and 1.4 in. thick. When rolled into place, it had to be done by two men because of its size and weight. It fit the tomb entrance perfectly because it had been hewn to fit like a cork in a bottle.

So why would God have designed such a precise method of burial? My assumptions go along some practical lines.

> The burial met all of Jewish traditional laws. The disciples could never be accused of faking the resurrection by hiding the body of Jesus. It took two men of impeccable integrity to handle the burial with precision. It took two men to move the stone into precise position covering the tomb entrance.
> Old Testament prophecy was exactly fulfilled. (Zechariah 12:10, Isaiah 53:9)

Do you know a Joseph or a Nicodemus in your life? That is a person that has been converted but can't go public because of political ties? It is predictable that there are some Christians that need to be quiet about their faith because of their roles in government. They need our prayers that they remain strong in their faith and that their principles are not threatened or compromised.

Pray especially for those members of the Supreme Court. It appears that Roe V. Wade could become a topic to be modified or abolished. Just think, perhaps in our lifetimes millions of unborn babies might live to become our leaders and citizens. Just maybe there are and could be members of the Supreme Court that are Joseph and or Nicodemus types that have been placed there by God through our votes at the presidential elections. It appears that we as Christians are called to vote as Jesus would vote.

So here we are with an often-overlooked detail of Jesus crucifixion and burial. Why would it be important to know the details? The obvious answer is that our God is a God of details. He is in total charge of all the decisions we make whether they be major or just minor actions. What a comfort to know that in all things God is involved in every occurrence of our lives. This story of Jesus burial gives me great comfort. How about you?

Prayer: Father, thanks you for giving us the security of telling us that that you are with us in all of the aspects of our lives. May we so live in honor and adoration of your presence. Amen

LISTEN OBEY AND TEACH

⁹ *"Only take care, and keep your soul diligently, lest you forget the things that your eyes have seen, and lest they depart from your heart all the days of your life. Make them known to your children and your children's children— ¹⁰ how on the day that you stood before the Lᴏʀᴅ your God at Horeb, the Lᴏʀᴅ said to me, 'Gather the people to me, that I may let them hear my words, so that they may learn to fear me all the days that they live on the earth, and that they may teach their children so.' ¹¹ And you came near and stood at the foot of the mountain, while the mountain burned with fire to the heart of heaven, wrapped in darkness, cloud, and gloom. ¹² Then the Lᴏʀᴅ spoke to you out of the midst of the fire. You heard the sound of words, but saw no form; there was only a voice. ¹³ And he declared to you his covenant, which he commanded you to perform, that is, the Ten Commandments,[a] and he wrote them on two tablets of stone. ¹⁴ And the Lᴏʀᴅ commanded me at that time to teach you statutes and rules, that you might do them in the land that you are going over to possess.*

Deuteronomy 4: 9-14

Moses is giving a speech of exhortation to Israel. In doing so, he wants them to take heed and obey. Moses wants the Israelites to remember how that their God has cared for them through the release from the cruel Pharaoh, crossing the Red Sea and all the other great stories of the Exodus.

Even though God has denied Moses entry into the promised land, Moses remains positive in his attitude. A lesson in attitude for us can be learned from Moses in that he does not show any negative behavior in being denied entry into the promised land. He seems content that he can visually see into the promised land, from the top of Mt. Nebo. It would have been expected that Moses would have pleaded with God to allow him entry after all he went through in leading the very negative people on the Exodus.

Some questions come to mind. Do your children know the spiritual impact that you experienced when you went through some of life's severe trials? Do they know where you stand politically and why? Of special interest are the spiritual issues that our country is experiencing. There is a definite culture shift taking place. If you fail to talk to your family about these issues, then they will probably adopt the issues of their professors in the college that they are attending.

Where are you in the spiritual leadership of your children? We can't afford to put off the conversations of how we as Christians view our changing culture. God instructed Moses to make sure that the Israelites would never forget their heritage of the Exodus and all the situations associated with the long trek.

The passing on of our roots and the trials of our lives need to be passed on to the next generation. We cannot leave this culture to change without our Christian influence upon our families.

Prayer:

> *America! America! God shed his grace on thee*
> *And crown thy good with brotherhood*
> *From sea to shining sea!*
> *Amen*

MILESTONES

I bore you on eagles' wings and brought you to myself.
⁵ Now therefore, if you will indeed obey my voice and
keep my covenant, you shall be my treasured
possession among all peoples, for all the earth is mine.
Exodus 19:4b-5

Fear not, for I have redeemed you; I have called you by
name, you are mine. When you pass through the
waters, I will be with you; and through the rivers, they
shall not overwhelm you; and when you walk through
the fire you shall not be burned, and the flames will not
consume you.

Isaiah 43: 1b-2

We all have experienced milestones in our lives that have borne special significance. These milestones have modified our attitudes, our way of thinking and even changed our actions. The typical milestones are mainly illnesses, untimely deaths, financial setbacks, marital discord just to name a few.

As of this writing, the entire earth is being inundated by a major milestone. It is a highly contagious virus called Covid-19. It started in China and has quickly spread across the entire globe. It is mainly spread by droplets from coughs and or sneezing. However, it lives on other surfaces for extended periods of time. So it is incumbent on society to wash hands often and to if possible, maintain at least a six foot space between others to minimize the possibility of air borne transmission.

The global incidence of infection is about 83 million people with approximately 1.8 million deaths. The medically challenged senior citizens are the most at risk because their ability to fight infections has become greatly diminished with age and/or underlying medical conditions. So federal and state government has stepped in and mandated the closure of public gatherings such as churches, schools, restaurants, sporting events etc. The financial hit of reduced revenues has hit restaurants, public transportation, lodging and airlines extremely hard.

This singular event is not only a milestone but is a global disaster such as the world has not experienced since the world wars or the great depression. Is God trying to get our attention? I have no doubt but that is certainly accurate! Just prior to the outbreak of the virus we were in a state of record making prosperity. Restaurants were crowded, portfolios were large, and churches were in many cases having difficulty in communicating the gospel to a culture that "had it made".

Now we need God. Maybe, just maybe, now is the time for America to come to the Lord. Today's scripture selection says to "fear not". God will bear us up on "eagles' wings". The next step is for us to recognize our need for the saving grace of God. Our only comfort in life and in death is that we are not our own but belong to our faithful savior Jesus Christ.

Prayer:

Father, we realize that we are not our own but we want to belong to you. Take us and mold us to be advocates for your kingdom, in sickness and in health, in riches or poverty, we are yours. Amen

MIRACLES

1 Therefore we must pay much closer attention to what we have heard, lest we drift away from it. 2 For since the message declared by angels proved to be reliable, and every transgression or disobedience received a just retribution, 3 how shall we escape if we neglect such a great salvation? It was declared at first by the Lord, and it was attested to us by those who heard, 4 while God also bore witness by signs and wonders and various miracles and by gifts of the Holy Spirit distributed according to his will.

Hebrews 2: 1-4

Webster's dictionary: a miracle is a supernatural event regarded as due to divine action.

It is within this indelible work of the Spirit in the lives of the saints that some have been selected to be miracle bearers. Yes, we still have miracles within our midst!

The reality of present miracles is readily observable through the eyes of faith. The miracles are within our present circles of friends and acquaintances. When we observe a miracle, we need to stop and ask "why". The answer is always the same, "so that you may believe".

My friend Leah was given months or less to live after her diagnosis of stage 4 endometrial cancer. That original diagnosis was three and one-half years ago. Leah is a miracle! She not only has a will to live but also has a will to serve. She said recently "I wonder what God has in store for me to do"?

The question one seldom hears is that "does God still do miracles"? We all know the answer to be absolutely "yes". If that is our response, then why are we so reticent to be vocal about the miracles around us? Could it be that we don't want to call a miracle for what it is just in case there might be a reversal of symptoms? Yes, we all will readily admit to the absolute certainty of death and taxes but we're not so sure about calling a miracle for what it so apparently is. Why not celebrate the miracles around us? Yes, the cancers in remission, the shrinking tumors, the person who was given 24 months to live but lived symptom free for 22 years (my first wife).

On a conversational level, we speak glowingly about a hole in one, a great catch of fish, the exciting winning touchdown but why do we not speak of the miracles around us? Of all the conversations for us to have the topic of miracles past and present are "steppingstones" to the mandated conversations that Jesus directed us to have just as he was about to ascend into heaven from his three-year ministry on earth. In Jesus words, "you'll receive power when the Holy Spirit has come upon you, and you'll be my witnesses in Jerusalem, and in all of Judea, Samaria and to the end of the earth". Acts 1:8

Prayer: Father, you have surrounded me with miracle healings, changed lives and people who will not call a miracle "a miracle" because it can't be scientifically explained. Give me the courage to open the conversational door that leads them to you. Amen

MOTORS

¹ Let brotherly love continue. ² Do not neglect to show hospitality to strangers, for thereby some have entertained angels unawares.

Hebrews 13:1-2

Calvin College, now University, in the 1950's, my future wife and I were babysitting two precious little girls under four years of age. After being put to bed, the youngest started to cry after only being in her bed for less than fifteen minutes. We both inquired "what's wrong"? Her response was "there's a mosquito in my room". We said, "how do you know, it's too dark in your room to see a mosquito." Her response has been often quoted, "I know he's here; I can hear his motor running."

By observation, we draw conclusions from our senses which aren't always accurate. Body size, dress, cleanliness etc. we reach conclusions as to what position they might have in life such as couch potato, runner, laborer, business executive etc.

Sensing is one of our gifts from God so that we can assess our environment. Factors to consider are personal safety in certain neighborhoods, comfortable appealing restaurants that "catch our eye" etc.

The mosquito was very present. Its motor was permanently shut off and our cute little gal was soon off to dreamland without noisy motors.

Our internal sensing capabilities are similar to an internal GPS and sonar like perceptions. These capacities allow us to evaluate personal safety in certain environments. The ability to perceive what might lie ahead is a fabulous tool to guard us upon life's journey.

In addition, based upon our past experiences and those or our circle of friends, we attempt to assess new acquaintances by sheer observation and either "write them off" or "give them a chance".

Speaking personally, I've been far too quick to make snap assessments when meeting new people. In some cases, I blush with shame for being so far off the mark. I didn't really give the new person(s) a chance. Summed up, I didn't give them a chance to "hear their motor running".

James 1:19 fits perfectly: Know this my beloved bothers: let every person be quick to hear, slow to speak, slow to anger.

Prayer: Father, give me a sensitive sense of fellow image bearers. I want to hear and sense their "running motors". Amen

NECESSARY

² And Paul went in, as was his custom, and on three Sabbath days he reasoned with of them from the Scriptures, ³ explaining and proving that it was necessary for the Christ to suffer and to rise from the dead, saying, "This Jesus, whom I proclaim to you, is the Christ."

Acts 17:2-3

Presently, all of the United States and in fact the globe is in various levels of lockdown. In the USA each state's governor has been in charge of establishing what needs to be done to minimize the spreading of the coronavirus. The impact of closed stores, churches, schools, sports at all levels is monumental. The Olympics have been rescheduled until 2021. NCAA March Madness was canceled as was all levels of professional sports. The economy has taken a severe downturn, thousands of workers have lost their jobs or have been laid off until the lockdown is terminated. As of this writing, it appears that the first of May will see stores and other business open up on a regional basis.

Essential business operations were allowed to stay open. Those qualifying were hospitals, grocery stores, liquor stores, marijuana stores, gas stations, abortion clinics and restaurant take-out only. This list is not all inclusive.

Some restricted areas caused a great deal of protest in Michigan were landscapers who couldn't begin their spring cleaning and planting and fishermen who couldn't launch their boats if they were motorized.

Very little protest was heard about the abortion clinics that were allowed to stay open because their operation was classified as essential.

We as Christians find ourselves in a unique situation. We are called upon by God to be active in explaining the gospel as the Apostle Paul was doing on three successive Sabbath days to the in the synagogue in Thessalonica. It was necessary to explain to the Jews that they were to hear the gospel first and then it would be explained to the gentiles.

It is necessary for each one of us to be ambassadors of the gospel. This is not open to a governor's edict. It is however necessary for the eternal destiny of those who we interact with more closely when the pandemic is behind us.

Prayer: Father listen to your children praying and witnessing to the eternal truth of the gospel. Amen

NEW EVERY MORNING

19 *Remember my affliction and my wanderings,*
the wormwood and the gall!
20 *My soul continually remembers it*
and is bowed down within me.
21 *But this I call to mind,*
and therefore I have hope:
22 *The steadfast love of the LORD never ceases;*[a]
his mercies never come to an end;
23 *they are new every morning;*
great is your faithfulness.
24 *"The LORD is my portion," says my soul,*
"therefore I will hope in him."

Lamentations 3: 19-24

I have a friend who I've known for a very long time who had something occur in his life during the recent coronavirus pandemic. He sent me an e-mail relating the story. It's rather long for this meditation, but it needs to be told in entirety.

Sam is my friend (not his real name because he wishes to remain anonymous.

Sam is very bright. He thinks like a college trained engineer but his actual background in education is heavy in economics.

Hydroponics is Sam's vocation. Totally self-taught, he has built greenhouses from scratch. Even the heating of the facilities had to be efficient. He built an offsite furnace in an old grain bin. He got the idea online from a Netherlands firm. All the directions were in Dutch. This didn't slow Sam's entrepreneurial mind. He built the furnace and piped the heat underground into the greenhouses where he had lettuce growing without soil with water and fertilizer controlled by computers.

The lettuce was beautiful as was the basil. The market was about two hours away in Green Bay. The business grew in that many cases of lettuce and herbs were delivered for sale in upscale markets and fine dining restaurants. Multiple loads per week and a growing business was standard.

Then the pandemic virus hit and state governors shut down restaurants except for take-out. Sam is making his last delivery to a produce distribution warehouse and meets up with a former buyer who has been promoted into management. He asks Sam about his business and Sam tells him it is almost down to nothing because of the mandated lockdown.

When Sam gets home he finds that suddenly his e-mails reflect that the buyers of produce are giving him much larger areas of shelf space in the fancy markets and business is now headed up instead of down.

In addition, Sam's workers at the greenhouses ask if he has ever advertised using online social media. Sam says, "No, but let's try it."

The result is that Sam now has so much demand that he can't grow lettuce and herbs fast enough.

Sam called me and said that today's scripture, especially verse 23 which states that God's faithfulness is new every morning has become a very special verse for him and his family. God blessed Sam's business beyond his wildest imagination. This is not to imply that God blesses his own because they are strong Christians. The point to be learned from the Sam story is that God does bless us out of sheer grace. During the viral pandemic, many business ventures were lost, even though the government stepped in and helped with the finances. God allowed the pandemic to bring our nation to an economic standstill. God was speaking to Sam before he blessed him. God continues to speak to Sam after revising his business plan. Today, Sam is thanking God by giving love to others and verbally telling others how God was so faithful to him and his family.

So where are you as readers? Is God in your lives? It is at times like this that God is talking to us and trying to get our attention. His faithfulness is new every morning. I urge you to put your trust in him. If God is not in your life now, why not call a Christian acquaintance. That person will listen to your story and direct you toward Jesus.

Prayer: Father listen to your children praying. May hearts be made accepting of your great plan of salvation. Yes, use me Father to be the friend that leads others to you. Amen

NO EXCUSES

¹The heavens declare the glory of God,
and the sky above proclaims his handiwork.
² Day to day pours out speech,
and night to night reveals knowledge.
³ There is no speech, nor are there words,
whose voice is not heard.
⁴ Their voice goes out through all the earth,
and their words to the end of the world.
In them he has set a tent for the sun,
⁵   which comes out like a bridegroom leaving his chamber,
and, like a strong man, runs its course with joy.
⁶ Its rising is from the end of the heavens,
and its circuit to the end of them,
and there is nothing hidden from its heat.

Psalm 19: 1-6

Consider yourself in the largest symphony hall in all the world with literally over 100 plus musicians in the orchestra. A choir of two to three hundred singers are there to complete the sound. From the opening downbeat of the director's baton, be prepared to be "blown away" by the magnificence of the sound. The heavens on a daily basis exceed even the most excellent musical experience you could ever imagine.

My wife likes to describe changing cloud formations. Her vivid imagination sees all kinds of figures in the clouds. She truly is a fan of God's creation.

The heavens depict the universal speech available to all of mankind. What a shame that so many of us just take the excellence of nature for granted.

What an opportunity to enter into a discussion with others about the assurance of eternity by beginning the conversation with" this is the day the Lord has made, let us rejoice and be glad in it". Ps. 118:24. My old friend Dave from Promise Keepers times referred to this verse from Psalm 118 and it left an impression upon my mind.

Wayne, my former hunting and fishing friend from Traverse City, who now calls Heaven home, and I made a weeklong trip to the Missoula, Montana area in search of rainbow trout. What struck me is that once we entered the majestic mountains Wayne started to whisper. He was overwhelmed with the majesty of creation. Yes, we also found rainbow trout in abundance that we promptly sent back to the Bitterroot River after enjoying their acrobatic antics at the ends of our fly-rods.

When surrounded with the majesty of God's creation, it is logical to conclude that man has no excuse for denying the existence of a God who created all this beauty. The Apostle Paul sums it all up in Romans 1:20

[20] *For his invisible attributes, namely, his eternal power and divine nature, have been clearly perceived, ever since the creation of the world, in the things that have been made. So they are without excuse.*

Prayer: We see you in nature. Your creation is mind-blowing. May we rejoice in your work by our words and actions. Amen

20 *"Behold, I send an angel before you to guard you on the way and to bring you to the place that I have prepared.* 21 *Pay careful attention to him and obey his voice; do not rebel against him, for he will not pardon your transgression, for my name is in him.*
22 *"But if you carefully obey his voice and do all that I say, then I will be an enemy to your enemies and an adversary to your adversaries.*
23 *"When my angel goes before you and brings you to the Amorites and the Hittites and the Perizzites and the Canaanites, the Hivites and the Jebusites, and I blot them out,* 24 *you shall not bow down to their gods nor serve them, nor do as they do, but you shall utterly overthrow them and break their pillars in pieces.* 25 *You shall serve the LORD your God, and he*[a] *will bless your bread and your water, and I will take sickness away from among you.* 26 *None shall miscarry or be barren in your land; I will fulfill the number of your days.* 27 *I will send my terror before you and will throw into confusion all the people against whom you shall come, and I will make all your enemies turn their backs to you.*

Exodus 23:20-27

When God was promising the Israelites the conquest of Canaan, he filled in all the possibilities. God sent a special angel to guard over them on their journey. God promised them that they would overcome any people group that might attempt to impede their trek. In addition, God promised them freedom from illness to the extent that even childbirth would go smoothly and that none would miscarry their unborn babies.

Presently, our entire globe is in hopefully the last throes of a viral siege named Covid 19. A pandemic is by definition a disease that engulfs the entire world. The entire economy was brought to a shuddering stand-still by the mandates to close public gatherings, schools churches etc. By definition only essential business was allowed to open. In Michigan, liquor stores, marijuana shops were considered essential. Essentially, the world's economy was bought to its "knees" in just a matter of weeks. At this writing, some six months after the onset of Covid 19, some schools have opted not to open in September. Sports will likely be halted or performed in stadiums closed to fans.

The pandemic started in China where it was allowed to progress, and global notification came in a belated fashion. Consequently, Covid 19 was already spreading globally because of air traffic, tourism and global business.

By contrast to how God made special travel plans for his chosen people before the exodus, one might ask where is God during our pandemic? The answer is quite simple. God hasn't moved. However, we as his image bearers have moved. We are in the process of figuratively building our own Tower of Babel. We have built this tower based upon our technology. Our mindset is that who needs God when we've got the internet? As of this writing, a spacecraft has been launched with Mars as its destination. The intent is to ascertain what fossils etc. can be brought back to validate the planet's formative years during evolution. Perhaps the findings might cause more questions than answers. One thing is for sure, the creator already has the answers to all of our questions.

Back to the pandemic and why? The answer is God allows difficult things to happen to us, his image bearers, to get our attention. We are not the captains of our own fates but are instead stewards of what God has entrusted to our care. So where are you in your thinking? If God delegated a special angel to watch over his people on their very difficult exodus, is he not also waiting for us to change our attitudes of we've got it made to worship the God of the universe?

Prayer: Father, may Covid 19 bring us to acknowledge you. It is your world, and we are only your humble servants. May our hearts be open to your leading and our following. Amen

PARABLES

Isaiah's Commission from the Lord:

8 And I heard the voice of the Lord saying, "Whom shall I send, and who will go for us?" Then I said, "Here I am! Send me." 9 And he said, "Go, and say to this people:

"'Keep on hearing, but do not understand;
keep on seeing, but do not perceive.'
10 Make the heart of this people dull,
and their ears heavy,
and blind their eyes;
lest they see with their eyes,
and hear with their ears,
and understand with their hearts,
and turn and be healed."
Isaiah 6: 8-10

10 And when he was alone, those around him with the twelve asked him about the parables. 11 And he said to them, "To you has been given the secret of the kingdom of God, but for those outside everything is in parables, 12 so that they may indeed see but not perceive, and may indeed hear but not understand, lest they turn and be forgiven."
Mark 4:10-12

Jesus, a master teacher, was remembered in three of the four gospels with an explanation of why the use of parables. Each gospel speaks to why Jesus used parables to explain his lessons to others. Just the fact that three gospels explained the use of parables is a statement which speaks to the importance of their use. Jesus' explanation is recorded in three gospels using almost identical language. Also, the similarity of Jesus' words to Isaiah's commission from the Lord underscores the importance of communicating clearly and effectively with the most important lessons of the gospel.

In my personal experience as a freshman high school student, I was assigned to take plane geometry as a core course. Math was not a strong suit for me. My past experience was that I had to dig explanations out of a textbook for algebra and let's just say that math was not one of my favorite subjects. My dread of the geometry class was totally unnecessary. My teacher, George Johnson, was a weekend National Guard helicopter pilot. He explained the angles and diagrams of geometry from 5,000 feet altitude and now I could visualize very readily the geometrical problems. Thanks to Mr. Johnson, geometry became alive for me because my teacher was speaking to me using parables and illustrations that I could visualize.

Part of my vocational experience as an elementary principal was to evaluate teachers as they were teaching. Without a doubt, the teachers that resonated with the children and were the most successful, were those that made liberal use of illustrations. They were using the parable method.

Back to Jesus, the master teacher. Jesus utilized parables so that the listeners could visualize and understand and remember. Needless to say, we need pastors and educators to make liberal use of illustrations and word pictures to make their teaching come alive.

Our lesson from Jesus is that we are his communicators. It is our job to let others know by our actions and words what the gospel is all about. So many of us have great attendance records at church services and Sunday School classes. However, head knowledge is just part of being a Christian. We need to communicate the gospel story in our actions and our speech. We are part of a team that is out on the front lines representing Jesus. Our presence might be the only way others might see Jesus. Our peers look to us to see what Christianity looks like. Now's the time for parables and illustrations.

Prayer: Father, forgive the times that I didn't represent you adequately when I had the opportunity. Give me a sensitivity to see others as possibly needing my witness. Also, help me to use illustrations that are meaningful and interesting for your kingdom. Amen

PARENTING

*12 As she continued praying before the L*ORD*,*
Eli observed her mouth.
13 Hannah was speaking in her heart; only her lips
moved, and her voice was not heard. Therefore Eli
took her to be a drunken woman.
14 And Eli said to her, "How long will you go on being
drunk? Put your wine away from you."
15 But Hannah answered, "No, my lord, I am a woman
troubled in spirit. I have drunk neither wine nor
strong drink, but I have been pouring out my soul
*before the L*ORD*.*
16 Do not regard your servant as a worthless woman,
for all along I have been speaking out of my great
anxiety and vexation."
17 Then Eli answered, "Go in peace, and the God of
Israel grant your petition that you have made to him."
18 And she said, "Let your servant find favor in your
eyes." Then the woman went her way and ate, and
her face was no longer sad.
I Samuel 1: 12-18

Hannah goes to God with her very fervent request for a
male child. She promises God that if he honors her
request, she will lend the child to the Lord. God honors
Hannah's request and she turns Samuel over to Eli for
mentoring and to later perform priestly duties for the
rest of his life. As an aside, God further honored this
devoted mother with other children after Samuel. Three
sons and two daughters followed.

Back to Eli. He rebukes his wayward sons who were
making a mockery out of their temple duties. They
carried on illicit affairs with whoever was available. In

addition, they profaned the peace offerings that were brought to the temple. They kept an inordinate amount of the offerings for their own personal consumption.

Eli reprimands his sons because temple worshipers reported back to Eli that his sons were out of control. Eli offers the following rebuke to his sons:

> 22 *Now Eli was very old, and he kept hearing that his sons were doing to all Israel, and how they lay with women who were serving at the entrance to the tent of meeting.*
> 23 *And he said to them, "why do you do such things? For I hear of your evil dealings from all these people.*
> 24 *No, my sons, it is no good report that I hear from the people of the Lord spreading abroad.*
> 25 *If someone sins against a man, God will mediate for him but if someone sins against the Lord, who can intercede for him? "But they would not listen to the voice of their father, for it was the will of the Lord to put them to death.*
> *I Samuel 2: 22-25*

God took the lives of Eli and his two sons in one day. The sons were killed in battle and Eli upon hearing the news fell over backwards and broke his neck.

We really do not have a clear scriptural explanation of how Hannah and Eli exhibited different parenting styles. It is very apparent that Eli was a very liberal parent whose sons were allowed to profane the temple with their outrageous behavior. Apparently, Eli had to be told by others that his sons were involved in very sinful practices. Eli should have intervened when his sons were in their formative years.

Conversely, Hannah and her family lived a godly life and God blessed her with a large family after her giving Samuel to the lord.

In our society, parenting is tough. Two incomes are the norm to maintain a standard of living that is quite necessary. The children are involved in sports at school and, are expected to be on various travel teams. Family meals are a thing of the past for the most part.

Parenting is difficult to say the least. Involve them with you in church attendance, be aware of what they are studying in school especially in public schools. Much of the curriculum has been very left leaning and anti-scriptural. Your solutions are to have knowledge and if you don't approve, attend board meetings. If communication with the board doesn't work you have charter, private, home and Christian schools as an option. You only have your children in the formative years for a very short time. Treat your parenting with prayer.

Prayer: Father, we are often confused with how to properly raise our children. May Hannah's example speak to us. Amen.

PASSING IT ON

⁵ For you, O Lord, are my hope,
my trust, O LORD, from my youth.
⁶ Upon you I have leaned from before my birth;
you are he who took me from my mother's womb.
My praise is continually of you.
⁹ Do not cast me off in the time of old age;
forsake me not when my strength is spent.
¹⁷ O God, from my youth you have taught me,
and I still proclaim your wondrous deeds.
¹⁸ So even to old age and gray hairs,
O God, do not forsake me,
until I proclaim your might to another generation,
your power to all those to come.
Psalm 71: 5,6,9,17,18

Current thinking in America does not value the wisdom associated with old age. Other countries typically respect and honor their senior citizens. This short meditation is not aimed at changing the perception of our culture regarding aging. It is however, a lesson for those who are in their autumn years to shift gears from "park" into "drive".

One of the least appreciated elements of modern society is the input from seniors that claim to have all the solutions to today's problems because they have lived through and solved similar problems.

Conversely, when asked by a member of the younger generation how to approach a problem, that is different because now we are being valued for our past experiences.

In fact, it is our mandate to proclaim how God has worked in our lives to another generation.

In prior times, seniors were more valued for their gained wisdom. Today's college educated millennials have been taught that America has a very negative heritage. As citizens of the USA we are expected to apologize for being members of a country that is the greatest civilization in history. So how are seniors supposed to let the next generation know what God has done in our lives?

How about relating the history of how America was founded? To find religious freedom was one of the major factors for their immigration. Acquainting our youth with the value of the constitution as written is another way to show our patriotic side. In addition, it needs to be pointed out that there are two schools of thought on how to interpret the constitution. One way is to take it in the language in which it was written. Another way is to make the constitution say things that are not in the document. An illustration is that the right to privacy is not found in the constitution. However, in 1973, The Supreme Court said that privacy was in the constitution and as a result 62 million babies have been murdered in vitro. Christians in name only are still supporting this American version of a fetal holocaust.

The list of what has happened in our lifetimes goes on. It is the duty of the older generation to let the younger generation know what some of the truths of American history are as told from a Christian vantage point.

Prayer: Father thank you for generational insights. Give us courage to not water down the truths of history to just be agreeable. Give us the wisdom to speak up for your kingdom when appropriate. Amen

RELATIONSHIPS

18 Then the Lord God said, "It is not good that the man should be alone; I will make a helper fit for him."
19 Now out of the ground the Lord had formed every beast of the field and every bird of the heavens and bought them to man to see what he would call them. And whatever the man had called every living creature, that was its name.
20 The man gave names to all livestock and to the birds of the heavens and to every beast of the field. But for Adam there was not found a helper fit for him.
21 So the Lord God caused a deep sleep to fall upon the man, and while he slept took one of his ribs and closed up its place with flesh.
22 And the rib that the Lord God had taken from the man he made her into a woman and brought her to the man.
23 Then the man said," This at last is bone of my bones and flesh of my flesh; she shall be called Woman, because she was taken out of man."
24 Therefore, a man shall leave his father and his mother and hold fast to his wife, and they shall become one flesh.

Genesis 2:18-24

God said that it was not good for man to be alone, so God made the first woman out of the flesh of the first man. Truly this was bone from bone and flesh from flesh. This was the first marriage, and it was truly not only arranged but it was made by God

Physical and caring relationships were initiated by God. Since this originally pure relationship started between Adam and Eve then sin entered into the world. At this moment of sin, the relationship with God changed as did the relationship between the newlyweds.

However, God was already planning ahead and said that the deliverance from sin would arrive in the person of his son Jesus Christ on the cross.

At the advent of sin, man's thinking was drastically altered. Man saw the world through the eyes of sin and at the same time man, because he was created in the image of God, he was capable of having loving relationships.

With the arrival of sin, the symptoms of sin also arrived. It didn't take long for the first homicide to occur, born out of sinful jealousy. God, being a holy God could not coexist with evil and so Cain was given a protective mark and sent away into the land of Nod.

Since those early days of being sent to the world's best garden, man has been plagued with all sorts of maladies, illness, strife, relationship deterioration, financial downturns, death etc.

The question is why does God inflict upon his image bearers such difficulties and trials? The obvious answer is that God wants to get our attention away from ourselves and to worship him. Some of us when faced with trials, purposely attempt to "get back at God". We have a mindset that that if God really loved us why would he allow such difficulties to enter our lives. Really? Since when have you become the director of the actions of a holy God? God wants you to come to him in worship and praise not in worship that lacks your heart and devotion.

If you can't get over what life has dealt you, God hasn't moved but you have. Now is a time to internally reconcile yourself to God and to come back to him.

David's story is a classic example of one who sinned by committing adultery and an arranged murder. God punished him by taking the lives of his sons. Yet David comes to God with a contrite heart in Psalm 51. If you need to ask forgiveness because of your negative attitude toward God, read Psalm 51 with special emphasis on verses 10 and 11. These verses are our closing prayer.

Create in me a clean heart, O God, and renew a right spirit within me. Cast me not away from your presence and take not your Holy Spirit from me. Amen

REVIVAL

The first recorded great revival began at Pentecost dated at about May, A.D.33. At that great revival, 3000 Jews came to Christ at the end of Peter's impassioned sermon. By the year 300, about 14 million had become Christians. By the year 500, this number has escalated to 40 million.

Peter's Pentecost Sermon Acts 2:14-41

Peter ends his sermon with the following verses found in Acts 2:38-41

38 Peter said to them, "Repent and be baptized, every one of you, in the name of Jesus Christ for the forgiveness of your sins, and you will receive the gift of the Holy Spirit. 39 The promise is for you and for your children and for all who are far off everyone for whom the Lord our God will call to himself."
40 And with many other words he bore witness and continued to exhort them, saying, "Save yourselves from this crooked generation." 41 So those who received his word were baptized, and there were added that day about three thousand souls.

Since the first great revival at the time of Pentecost there have several others. The First Great Awakening took place in the American colonies in the early 1700's. Great preachers such as Jonathan Edwards and the silver-tongued orator, George Whitefield led the movement.

Meanwhile, in England John Wesley was active in initiating the Wesleyan Revival. At Wesley's death there were 79,000 Methodists in England and 40,000 in America.

The Second Great Awakening began at the Cane Ridge camp meeting in Kentucky in 1801. During this same time, five students from Williams College in Massachusetts were praying under a haystack to take cover from a thunderstorm. This Haystack Prayer Meeting was later know as the beginning of America's foreign missions in that four of the five students spent their entire working lives in overseas' missions.

In New York City, in 1851, six people met to pray. This began The Prayer Meeting Revival. Over a million people devoted their lives to Jesus Christ. Over a million people in England also became converts.

The Welsh Revival began in 1904 and it added 100,000 converts to the Welsh Church. An offshoot of this revival was the start of Pentecostalism which began in the Azusa Street Revival in Los Angeles.

China banned Christian missionaries in 1953. However, in 1980 the number of Christians had grown to 2 Million. By the year 2,000, the number had jumped to 75 million. Isn't it amazing that in times of duress and oppressive government, Christianity has exploded?

Right now a global pandemic called coronavirus is rampaging. There is no real therapeutic medicine. So social isolation, quarantine and a soon available vaccine are the only preventative measures that are available. Churches, social gatherings of more than 10 are banned, many business establishments are shut down and many are failing financially. All sports are in lockdown. March Madness has been cancelled. The 2020 Summer Olympics scheduled for Japan will be postponed until 2021.

The United States Congress has voted in a two trillion-dollar rescue plan to help failing business ventures and to give a financial stipend to families that have been stripped of their livelihood. It is not known when the lockdown restrictions can be lifted. As of this writing, the President is hoping to begin opening some business areas by around Easter.

Who would have thought that the healthy economy of our country could be brought to its knees by an elusive virus? Being on our knees in prayer is certainly indicated. Why not meet over some coffee when the threat has weakened and having prayer as a key ingredient instead of the usual more trivial topics. Who knows, perhaps this might be the spark of another Great Awakening.

Prayer: Father, the familiar passage found in Chronicles 7:14 comes to mind:

> *If my people, who are called by my name.*
>
> *Will humble themselves and pray and seek*
>
> *my face and turn from their wicked ways,*
>
> *then will I hear from heaven and will*
>
> *forgive their sin and will heal their land.*
>
> *Amen*

SENIOR MINISTRY

1 Do not rebuke an older man but encourage him as you would a father, younger men as brothers,
2 older women as mothers, younger women as sisters, in all purity.
3 Honor the widows who are truly widows.
4 But if a widow has children or grandchildren, let them first learn to show godliness to their own household and to make some return to their parents, for this is pleasing in the sight of God.
5 She who is truly a widow, left all alone, and has set her hope on God and continues in supplications and prayers night and day,
6 but she who is self-indulgent is dead even while she lives.
7 Command these things as well, so that they may be without reproach.
8 But if anyone does not provide for his relatives, and especially for members of his household, he has denied the faith and is worse than an unbeliever.
I Timothy 5:1-8

Paul writes to his spiritual son, Timothy. He issues some fatherly advice about how a church should be sensitive to the needs of their senior citizens. This group of retirees are often overlooked and because we know something about them, we assume that their needs are all being met.

As an aside, Timothy was not a church pastor at Ephesus. He was a church leader who relied heavily upon Paul's mentorship. Paul's letter to Timothy takes place when the church at Ephesus is being plagued with many false teachers.

Currently, in this day of self-sufficiency, we can learn from Paul's insight into the possible needs of the church's seniors.

In today's society there is an assumption that because we have a general idea of a senior's situation on a spiritual, financial and physical level that we think their needs are being met. Paul in his letter to Timothy, is basically saying, "don't assume you know about your seniors just because you see them in worship.

If the senior has family ties available to them let the family meet the needs of their grandparents and parents.

However, to those seniors who are alone, the church needs to be "on top" of their needs. They need to know their needs on a physical, financial and spiritual level. Other seniors who do not have many needs are an excellent source of volunteers who can visit and call the seniors that are alone. Bear in mind that being alone is only one area of potential need. Some senior couples might just need some assistance too.

Are there health needs?
Do they need transportation to appointments and shopping?
Does their property need repair?
Are there cognition problems?
Are they lonely and perhaps need a visit?
Do they have an alert system?
Is their neighborhood safe?

Perhaps you have some ideas as to what can be done in your church. Why not communicate with the church deacons and let them know.

Prayer: Father so often we overlook those in need because we aren't aware. Give us a sense of reaching out to those seniors that just might need someone to talk to or to offer to give them a ride etc. Amen

SIGNS

The blood shall be a sign for you, on the houses where you are. And when I see the blood, I will pass over you, and no plague will befall you to destroy you, when I strike the land of Egypt.

Exodus 12:13

37 Now when they heard this they were cut to the heart, and said to Peter and the rest of the apostles, "Brothers, what shall we do?"
38 And Peter said to them, "Repent and be baptized every one of you in the name of Jesus Christ for the forgiveness of your sins, and you will receive the gift of the Holy Spirit.
39 For the promise is for you and for your children and for all who are far off, everyone whom the Lord our God calls to himself."

Acts 2:37-39

We experience signs in our culture to the point of overkill. We have billboards, electronic billboards, traffic signs, business signs etc. We literally have so many signs that they take away from the raw beauty of the countryside.

Football and baseball would be a disaster without signs being exchanged between coaches and players. Referees and umpires communicate with known signs to communicate their decisions.

Even protests and parades carry signs to get their messages across to the crowds watching their parades.

Toward the end of Jesus' ministry, the Jews were asking for more signs from Jesus which was basically a stalling technique. The gospel had been clearly preached and instead of saying yes or no to the gospel, they hesitated and asked for more signs. They didn't need any additional signs. What they needed was to make a decision for Jesus.

The Greeks were more authentic. They were the students of the times. They truly wanted more wisdom.

The question really is the same for both Jews and Greeks, "what are you going to do with the gospel of Jesus?"

The Jewish tradition of celebrating the Passover is still being done. It is a major time of remembering the exodus from Egypt to the Promised Land but especially the blood of a lamb over the doorposts of each home.

We also have times of special celebrations remembering the birth of Jesus, his resurrection and the indwelling of the Holy Spirit. These are signs of the gospel and are more important than the other signs around us. These days of celebration are perfect times to invite a friend or a neighbor to worship with us and even to sit with us during worship.

In addition to all the signs and special days recorded in the Bible, there are many signs that take place in our own personal lives. Many of us have experienced miraculous healings, recovery from financial problems, recovery of our home life by improved conditions etc.

The overarching question is the same as was summarized in Peter's great Pentecost sermon, "repent and be baptized and you will receive the gift of the Holy Spirit."

Do you need more signs? No, it's decision time. What will you do with the plan of salvation? Regardless of your past, Jesus will forgive your confessed sins and accept you into his growing family. May God bless your decision.

Prayer: Father, forgive my sins of the past. I love you and will give you my best for the rest of my life. Amen

SLUGGARD

⁶ Go to the ant, O sluggard;
consider her ways, and be wise.
⁷ Without having any chief,
officer, or ruler,
⁸ she prepares her bread in summer
and gathers her food in harvest.
Proverbs 6: 6-8

An opening scene of my early education took place in a one room Christian grade school which housed grades 1-8. My desk was right next to the door which opened directly to the outside. It was a wood door with the upper one half composed of glass.

Our teacher was a middle-aged man who was slightly built but had a booming voice. One of the more unruly students (an eighth grader) angered our teacher/principal. Apparently, Clyde hadn't turned in his homework and was not about to get busy and complete his assignments. The teacher lost it and in his very loudest voice quoted directly from Proverbs and aimed directly at Clyde "go to the ant thou sluggard; consider her ways and be wise."

Clyde wasn't about to take the role of being a sluggard, so he ran to the exit door and slammed it with such force that my desk was littered with shattered window glass. This was quite a traumatic moment in the life of a shy five year old.

Even though at the time I had no idea what a sluggard was, I made a pact within myself to never become one.

Now, decades later I can still recall the incident as if it were yesterday.

As each of us looks back upon our lives and the events that made an indelible mark upon us we probably can readily bring up events that have shaped us and caused us to think and shape our thinking. As Psalm 90:12 says, "so teach us to number our days that we may get a heart of wisdom." It appears that the incidents that we recall that shaped our behaviors and thinking were part of the process of numbering our days.

A simple definition of what it means to number our days is to pay attention to the various events of our lives that we have lived through and that God has watched over us. Think back how has God preserved your life and watched over you?

Prayer: Father you have brought us to this point in each one of our lives and we give you thanks for watching over us. You have given us opportunities to let others know how you are in charge of our days. We number them and give you all the glory. Amen

11. I saw that under the sun the race is not to the swift, nor the battle to the strong, nor bread to the wise, nor riches to the intelligent, nor favor to those with knowledge, but time and chance happen to them all.

12. For man does not know his time. Like fish are taken in an evil net, and like birds that are caught in a snare, so the children of man are snared at an evil time, when it suddenly falls upon them.
Ecclesiastes 9:11-12

We have no idea how God measures time. We do know however that he is unwavering in keeping his promises. The promises of God are absolutes. It all started in the Garden of Eden with Adam and Eve violating God's command and sure enough, God's judgement was immediate in that they were expelled from the garden to a life of sweaty toil and eventual mortal death.

Now we wait for the second coming of Jesus. At that time our present existence will end and we will be caught up to our eternal home with our resurrected bodies. We don't know when but we do know that it will happen absolutely on God's unpublished time schedule.

Every one of us who has raised a family is familiar with the rhetoric from the backseat, "are we there yet." As children we have an immature conception of time. We just can't wait for Christmas, our birthday, school to end, school to start etc.

During our adult life, it seems like the years are going by faster. Before we know it, our kids ae raised and we are "empty nesters". Life has gone by in a blur.

It is during this latter part of our working years that we become more aware of our mortality. We take more seriously the words of Psalm 90 which speaks of our life spans.

10 The years of our lives are seventy, or even by reason of strength eighty; yet their span is but toil and trouble; they are soon gone, and we fly away.
12 So teach us to number our days that we may get a heart of wisdom

Our retirement finally comes, and we start emptying our bucket list of the things we have been putting off. We travel, maybe volunteer, spend more time with the grandchildren, and in general we attempt to give back in other creative ways.

When you enter the last chapter of your life, may you have the assurance that heaven will be your final destination. A friend of mine knew that his days were numbered in single digits and he has since passed on into glory. We tried to visit him over our traditional annual lunch, but Dick wasn't up to it. His wife said maybe a desert might be fine with a cup of joe. So three old buddies delivered cherry pie which was "just right" for our friend. Before we could even finish the "small talk" Dick said, "I want you guys to stop praying for my healing. I'm coming around third and I'm beginning my slide home and I'm coming in "spikes up". So don't, don't block the plate.

That is the positive assurance that we all need to have when we round third. Where are you at with Jesus? He is standing at the plate and is waiting.

Prayer: Lord may we utilize your time which you have allocated for us with a positive hope for salvation. Amen

STRESS

Stress is probably one of the leading factors that affects our mental and physical lives. It is present in each one of our lives. It is perceived by each individual in their own unique way.

Some of us experience stress that is job related. This can be caused by demanding management, negative working conditions as shown by fellow workers that are negative about most job-related conditions. Solutions to stress might be to meet with management one on one and seek reasons and/or changes.

Marital stress is very difficult to deal with. Solutions might begin with honest in-depth conversations between spouses. Sometimes entire families need to sit down and "clear the air". The sources of stress are endless. In fact, many experience stress and are totally oblivious to it being present.

As an aside, we as Christians need to be sensitive to the needs of others that may be overwhelmed with stress. We just might observe one of our friends acting out in an "over the top" manner. This behavior could be stress related. This might be an opportunity to meet for a cup of coffee and a friendly conversation.

This past Labor Day was a wonderful time of meeting with my extended family around a backyard pool. Good conversation sprinkled the day and one topic was that of stress. We all agreed that stress was present in all of our lives and that people deal with stress in a multitude of ways. Some receive medication, others medicate themselves and some exercise or watch television or read. My grandson, a medical doctor concluded the conversation with a quotation take from Matthew 6. He stated that when followed, it is the only real cure for the handling of stress. We all agreed. My unanswered question is why isn't the cure for stress the first solution that we reach out to? Perhaps this observation might be a good topic for you and your friends and/or family to discuss.

25 Therefore, I tell you, do not be anxious about your life, what you will eat or what you will drink, nor about your body, what you will put on. Is not life more than food, and the body more than clothing?
26 Look at the birds of the air: they neither sow nor reap nor gather into barns, and yet your heavenly Father feeds them, are you not of more value than they?
27 And which of you by being anxious can add a single hour to his span of life?
28 Why are you anxious about clothing? Consider the lilies of the field, how they grow: they neither toil nor spin,
29 Yet I tell you, even Solomon in all his glory was not arrayed like one of these.
30 But if God so clothes the grass of the field, which today is alive and tomorrow is thrown into the oven, will he not much more clothe you, O you of little faith?
31 Therefore do not be anxious, saying, "What shall we eat"? Or "what shall drink?" or "What shall we wear?"
32 For the Gentiles seek after all these things, and your heavenly Father knows that you need them all.
33 But seek first the kingdom of God and his righteousness, and all these things will be added to

you.
[34] Therefore do not be anxious about tomorrow, for tomorrow will be anxious for itself. Sufficient for the day is its own trouble.

Matthew 6:25-34

Prayer: Father we all have situations in our lives that give us anxiety. We ask that your promises of divine care will give us a peace from our cares. Amen

TATTOO

What! My grandson, a medical doctor, taking a residence in Family Practice, has a tattoo on his arm. I had to see for myself and upon seeing him in a short-sleeved shirt, the tat was a scripture verse:

May I never boast except in the cross of our Lord Jesus Christ, through which the world has been crucified to me, and I to the world.

Galatians 6:14

After examining the tat, I asked my grandson what was his rationale in getting tattooed? His reply was simply, "as you know Grandpa, I'm planning on practicing medicine among people that are in poorer neighborhoods in a Christian clinic. My calling is that as a physician, to minister to the physical bodies of my patients but when they ask about my tattoo, the ice has been broken and I'll have an opportunity to minister to the health of their soul.

After my conversation with my doctor grandson, I was internally grateful that I hadn't called him and denounced that how can a doctor have a tattoo and maintain an aura of respectability? God spared my tongue and he opened my heart and I learned another lesson of listening before becoming judgmental.

My generation has a tendency to readily condemn and is slow to listen. We are too set in our ways to consider that God wants us to be all things to all people. We are not given a scriptural mandate to be salt and light to only those people who look and act just like us.

So where are you in your analysis of your own personal mission field? Are you perhaps prejudging and categorizing others that need to hear your gospel invitation and "writing them off" before you give them a chance?

Prayer: Father, give me a zeal to see others as you see them and bring them the good news of salvation without "walking to the other side of the road" and avoiding them. Amen

TEACHING

4 "Hear, O Israel: The LORD our God, the LORD is one.
5 You shall love the LORD your God with all your heart
and with all your soul and with all your
might. 6 And these words that I command you today
shall be on your heart. 7 You shall teach them diligently
to your children, and shall talk of them when you sit in
your house, and when you walk by the way, and when
you lie down, and when you rise. 8 You shall bind them
as a sign on your hand, and they shall be as frontlets
between your eyes. 9 You shall write them on the
doorposts of your house and on your gates.

Deuteronomy 6: 4-9

The opening statement in today's scripture is called the Shema. Orthodox Jews voice the Shema morning and night. The meaning is that there is only one God and that there are no rivals.

Parents in Israel take parenting very seriously. When the family dines together, they make sure that the conversation includes God, the Exodus and all their God led past.

In our modern society it is very difficult for a family to enjoy a meal together. Our lives are filled with activities such as school functions, school sports, music, robotics etc. However, when we do have a meal together it would be a great opportunity to relate stories of how God has led us as individuals and as a family. If we as parents avoid the chances to share, the memories of God's providential leadership will fade into oblivion.

As a parent, what are the happenings in your personal life and family history that has shaped your life? Does your spouse know your story? Do your children know your history? If we as parents aren't open with our histories, then we are missing a great opportunity to share our faith.

The Covid-19 virus is now overwhelming the global state of health both physical and financial and is forcing families to stay home, become unemployed and establish a near quarantine type of existence. Schools are cancelled, including all their activities, churches are shut down, restaurants are limited to take out orders, all national and regional sports are cancelled. Television is showing historical sports activities and spending copious amount of time explaining the virus that has afflicted us and generally spreading fear to the listeners.

So, we are at home. Our options are reading, old movies, old sports and "oh my" what are we going to do with our time? How about talking to each other?

What an opportunity to tell our stories. How did mom and dad meet and later marry? How did we grow up? How did we come to know and love Jesus? How did God save me in that great illness that is now in remission? How about that terrifying chain reaction traffic accident that left me with no car but with a non-injured body?

As you read this meditation, the memory of a Covid-19 virus is hopefully fading, jobs have been restored, church activities have been restored and hopefully reenergized, schools are back in session and you are sitting thinking about your own personal exodus from the near depression. Give thanks! God has spared us and now we need to add another paragraph to our story. Are you up to it?

Prayer: Father, we feel that we are living in the end times. We don't know the future, but rest assured that you hold the future. May we be faithful in telling our stories about how we love you. Amen

THE ALMIGHTY

¹ When Abram was ninety-nine years old the Lord appeared to Abram and said to him, "<u>I am God Almighty</u>; walk before me, and be blameless".
Genesis 17:1

¹⁰ And God said to him, "Your name is Jacob; no longer shall your name be called Jacob, but Israel shall be your name." So he called his name Israel. ¹¹ And God said to him, "I am God Almighty: be fruitful and multiply. A nation and a company of nations shall come from you, and kings shall come from your own body.
Genesis 35:10-11

God introduces himself when we are in need as the Almighty. When Abraham was 99 years old God assured him by name (the Almighty) that he would be a father of a multitude of nations.

Jacob had God's promise ringing in his ears when God said" I am the God Almighty". The land that was given to Abraham is now again promised to continue to Jacob's offspring.

He who abides in the shelter of the Most High will abide in the shadow of the Almighty.
Psalm 91:1

Because you have made the Lord your dwelling place—the Most High who is my refuge–no evil shall be allowed to befall you, no plague come near your tent.

For he will command his angels concerning you to guard you in all your ways Psalm 91: 9-11

We are promised the shelter of God the Almighty in Psalm 91:1. What a wonderful psalm of comfort and promise when we are faced with life's difficulties.

"I am the Alpha and the Omega," says the Lord God, who is and who was and who is to come, the Almighty. Revelation 1:8

Hallelujah! For the Lord our God the Almighty reigns. Revelation 19:6b

Looking ahead to the book of Revelation, God is assuring us of his existence from the beginning (Alpha) to the end (Omega). Again, we are reminded that he is the Almighty. Never in our lives and the lives of all who ever lived has anyone been without the presence of the Almighty. The Almighty can't be explained in human terms. It can only be experienced in our present mortal lives and in our future immortal lives that will exist for all eternity. So in terms of today's language, the Almighty not only has our back, in fact he has our all. The unanswered question is: does the Almighty have your all?

Prayer: Father Almighty, I pledge myself anew to you today. You are my all in all. Amen

THE PURPOSE OF THE PARABLES

10 Then the disciples came and said to him, "Why do you speak to them in parables?" 11 And he answered them, "To you it has been given to know the secrets of the kingdom of heaven, but to them it has not been given. 12 For to the one who has, more will be given, and he will have an abundance, but from the one who has not, even what he has will be taken away. 13 This is why I speak to them in parables, because seeing they do not see, and hearing they do not hear, nor do they understand. 14 Indeed, in their case the prophecy of Isaiah is fulfilled that says:

"""You will indeed hear but never understand,
and you will indeed see but never perceive."
15 For this people's heart has grown dull,
and with their ears they can barely hear,
and their eyes they have closed,
lest they should see with their eyes
and hear with their ears
and understand with their heart
and turn, and I would heal them.'

Matthew 13: 10-15

In my time spent as an elementary principal, it was my pleasure to observe the different teaching styles of various teachers. Some styles were very much in step with textbooks and study guides where all the students were expected to all be "on the same page". However, one of my more successful teachers began to individualize her approach to teaching in that she met each child where they were at and then taught them in their comfort and understanding zone. Wow, the difference was soon noticed by other teachers and they too began to individualize their teaching methods.

Jesus utilized parables to enhance understanding. When the disciples questioned his use of parables, Jesus basically said that illustrations were necessary to enhance understanding. The use of parables was recorded in three of the gospels thus giving emphasis to the attraction of their use in connecting with the people. Also, Jesus was followed by crowds of people. Without a doubt they were in love with this teacher that healed and spoke in a language that met them where they were.

For those of us in the communication areas of education and church ministry, we can learn from Jesus the master teacher. Churches that are attracting increasing numbers of members are those that preach the Word of God in clarity and truth. Schools that have great reputations in the community are the ones that stick to the basics.

When we think back over the years of our favorite preachers and memorable teachers, I believe that we remember best those that used illustrations (parables). What a lesson for all of us who want to connect with others.

The main point of this meditation is that as followers of Jesus, we have a message of salvation to impart to those people that we interact with. Now it's time to be intentional in getting our message across. It is time to use some illustrations. (parables)

Prayer: Father, when the Spirit nudges me to share your gospel, give me clarity of thought and illustrations that will speak to hearts. Amen

THE TRUE VINE

15 *"I am the true vine, and my Father is the vinedresser. 2 Every branch in me that does not bear fruit he takes away, and every branch that does bear fruit he prunes, that it may bear more fruit. 3 Already you are clean because of the word that I have spoken to you. 4 Abide in me, and I in you. As the branch cannot bear fruit by itself, unless it abides in the vine, neither can you, unless you abide in me. 5 I am the vine; you are the branches. Whoever abides in me and I in him, he it is that bears much fruit, for apart from me you can do nothing. 6 If anyone does not abide in me he is thrown away like a branch and withers; and the branches are gathered, thrown into the fire, and burned. 7 If you abide in me, and my words abide in you, ask whatever you wish, and it will be done for you. 8 By this my Father is glorified, that you bear much fruit and so prove to be my disciples. 9 As the Father has loved me, so have I loved you. Abide in my love. 10 If you keep my commandments, you will abide in my love, just as I have kept my Father's commandments and abide in his love. 11 These things I have spoken to you, that my joy may be in you, and that your joy may be full.*

John 15:1-11

Lately, I have been "on a tear" according to my peers and children. It all started with the removal of some rather diseased and stately pine trees. Their removal left a glaring lack of privacy. To regain some privacy by planting replacement trees will be a very slow process and one which I will never see because of my many years on earth. So, I'm planting fast growing privacy shrubs and replacement flowers to disguise the lawn scars left by removed trees. This dilemma has minimized my time on the waters doing a far more enjoyable activity called fishing.

Jesus spoke in parables for clarity of his message to his followers and disciples. In today's parable regarding the vine, I'm thinking of well-tended grapes that are in rows, tied to uprights and irrigated by an automatic irrigation system. As one travels though wine country it illustrates quite clearly what Jesus was talking about when he said that he was the true vine and his Father the vinedresser. When we are in Christ, we are branches that get our nourishment through the vine. The vinedresser is always assessing the quality of the branches. Pruning is absolutely necessary for the branches to bear more fruit. In addition, pruning is essential to eliminate dying and diseased branches.

In today's society of technology which is rated on one's efficiency but also on the speed of delivery we are assessed by our peers and others regarding our value in the workplace. It is easy to blend our work assessment with our spiritual life. This can be confusing and causes us to do some spiritual introspection on an individual level. Good intentions are not enough. What really counts is our spiritual fruit. That fruit is the impact that we have and are making by our words and lifestyles. Are we making a difference or are we just going along with the crowd of spiritual mediocrity?

Our heavenly Father is looking at our worth as a spiritual branch. The pruning process might involve financial change, marital problems, health changes etc. It is only when we as branches are pruned by the vinedresser that we bear more fruit. Where are you as a branch that is part of the vine called Jesus?

Prayer: Father, I'm looking at my health on a spiritual level. Give me a clear understanding of where I am as a part of the vine. Amen

TIME TO THINK

Finally, brothers, whatever is true, whatever is honorable, whatever is just, whatever is pure, whatever is lovely, whatever is commendable, if there is any excellence, if there is anything worthy of praise, think about these things.

Philippians 4:8

When do you have time to think in depth? Our society is driven to seek out things that perform for us at faster paces than what we presently work with and enjoy. Some items become obsolete especially in the arena of technology and we are motivated to invest in items that perform tasks more efficiently and in less time.

Demand is created for:

1. Faster internet
2. TV streaming with or without ads
3. Cars that almost drive for us.
4. Remote control of our electrical appliances

The list goes on and on. Recently, over dinner with a grandson and his wife, he posed a question "what are you doing for your devotional time? Great question for a fast-paced society. I suspect that many of us have abbreviated times to get alone with our thoughts and with God. I know that my personal time of devotional thinking has peaks and valleys. When life is smooth, my meditation time suffers. When difficulties come my way, my devotional life deepens and gets more focused.

How about right now. Take a brief "time out" to ask yourself the question if you're taking the time to think about what is honorable, just, pure, lovely, commendable, excellence, worthy of praise.

Think about these things.

Prayer: Father, forgive my abbreviated and or missing times that I'm spending in your word and prayer. Teach me the lesson of being content with where I'm at right now. Amen

TRACKING

14 Bless those who persecute you; bless and do not curse them. 15 Rejoice with those who rejoice, weep with those who weep. 16 Live in harmony with one another. Do not be haughty, but associate with the lowly. Never be wise in your own sight. 17 Repay no one evil for evil, but give thought to do what is honorable in the sight of all. 18 If possible, so far as it depends on you, live peaceably with all. 19 Beloved, never avenge yourselves, but leave it to the wrath of God, for it is written, "Vengeance is mine, I will repay, says the Lord." 20 To the contrary, "if your enemy is hungry, feed him; if he is thirsty, give him something to drink; for by so doing you will heap burning coals on his head." 21 Do not be overcome by evil, but overcome evil with good.

Romans 12:14-21

Hunting with my son and his sons is a high point of my role as a father and grandfather. Hunting consists of picking a likely spot for game to appear. However, tracking is the key to find that best spot for deer to visit. Veteran hunters can "read" the signs of deer movement and habits. Hunters who are very successful track their game prior to the onset of the hunting season and are prepared to wait for the deer to appear on opening day.

In the above scripture we are given all kinds of advice on how to interact. Our actions are to "track" others in a way that is sensitive to their needs. So there is a time to weep and a time to laugh. In so doing, we can empathize with others and show our love and witness. So when you are "tracking" others you are being sensitive. You "are there for them". "You have their back". Never should you gossip to others the confidences shared during your times of consoling hurting people. Instead, you sit with them, you listen without sharing the woes of others including those of your own. Listening is the key to spiritual tracking. Only by your presence can we really listen. Cards, texts and e-mails are better than no contact but your presence, your listening, and your empathy is the ultimate way to "being there for them".

The next level of "tracking" is to "bend over backwards for the "hard to love". These are the people that have lost their smile years ago. They are judgmental and demanding. So now is the time to "heap burning coals on their heads". All we can do is love them to the best of our capabilities and leave the judgmental decisions up to God.

This "tracking" of others in need isn't easy. In fact, many times it causes us great internal discomfort. However, many times that we dread are often turned into times of internal blessing when we "were there" for the hard to love person.

Prayer: Father, forgive me and my judgmental mind and give me a loving heart that reaches out to others that need you through me and my loving visit. Amen

UNDER CONSTRUCTION

10 According to the grace of God given to me, like a skilled master builder I laid a foundation, and someone else is building upon it. Let each one take care how he builds upon it.
11 For no one can lay a foundation other than that which is laid, which is Jesus Christ.
12 Now if anyone builds on the foundation with gold, silver, precious stones, wood, hay, straw—
13 each one's work will become manifest, for the Day will disclose it, because it will be revealed by fire, and the fire will test what sort of work each one has done.
14 If the work that anyone has built on the foundation survives, he will receive a reward.
15 If anyone's work is burned up, he will suffer loss, though he himself will be saved, but only as through fire.
16 Do you not know that you are God's temple and that God's Spirit dwells in you?
17 If anyone destroys God's temple, God will destroy him. For God's temple is holy, and you are that temple.
I Corinthians 3: 10-17

Being a bachelor at age 74 was a unique experience for me. My wife of 54 blessed years went on to her eternal reward of glory. After about three months of keeping myself busy with interior painting of my home, my daughter gave me some sage advice: "Dad why don't you do some woodworking. When my boys were younger, they spent hours on the rocking horse that you built?" So I proceeded to outfit a workshop in the unfinished basement of my home.

A good friend, who had much more experience in working with wood became my mentor, my close friend, more accurately my soul mate. We even finished a dining room table for my daughter in law. It only took three years of laughter, marginal language and finally some exclamations of approval. Table completed!

Spiritually, we are all examples of what our lives should look like under construction. When we adhere to God's Word for our lives, things go along much more smoothly.

The Apostle Paul in today's scripture gives a wonderful example of what our earthly temples (bodies) should look like. If you are able, align yourself with a soul mate with whom you can confidentially share your thoughts, doubts, hopes, goals, failures etc. We are all "under construction" and the temple in which you reside needs to be measured, sized, planed, sawn and appraised by another set of eyes and ears. (Your soul mate)

The table is now completed. However, the temple is still under construction and needs some constructive changes. How's your temple going? You are a holy creation and God lives within you. Your family and peers are observing and listening, and some are following your example. You just might be the "construction foreman". Are you up to it?

Prayer: Father, today I'm evaluating my temple. It's not perfect. I ask for your Spirit to work within me and plane me to be a sharper temple image. Amen

WALLS

17 Then I said to them, "You see the trouble we are in, how Jerusalem lies in ruins with its gates burned. Come, let us build the wall of Jerusalem, that we may no longer suffer derision."
18 And I told them of the hand of my God that had been upon me for good, and also of the words that the king had spoken to me. And they said, "Let us rise up and build." So they strengthened their hands for the good work.
Nehemiah 2: 17,18

We build walls for our own safety. In Southern California most subdivisions come with a completed cinder block wall which encloses the entire back yard. More exclusive communities are gated which constitutes a wall that is not visual.

The governor's mansion in Michigan is having an 8ft. electrified fence installed. This hopefully will keep out the uninvited.

The USA / Mexico border is being bordered by a huge wall. This is an attempt to keep out undocumented immigrants.

In the book of Revelation, the New Jerusalem has a four-sided wall which extends 1,380 miles in length, width and height. (Can't wait to see that)

The time of Nehemiah is concurrent with the great Persian Empire. Cyrus the Great is the one in charge. The date is about 450 B.C. Cyrus gives Nehemiah permission to go check out the wall of Jerusalem and see the wall for himself. He is an optimist and tells Cyrus that the Israelites can rebuild the wall by themselves. Cyrus agrees to this plan. It doesn't cost his empire a red cent and he doesn't have to use any of his own construction guys to get the job done.

The Israelites are organized by family units. Each unit is assigned to rebuild a particular part of the wall. Give Nehemiah credit as a great administrator in that it only takes 52 days to complete the project. (Nehemiah 6:15)

Then the celebration, called the Feast of Booths takes place. Ezra, the priest read the law of Moses to the people. They are overwhelmed with the reading and they weep tears of joy. The celebration lasts an entire week. During this time of celebration and worship the people bow down and raise their arms in reverence and joy.

Each one of us builds inner personal walls. Typically, these walls are based upon personal bias. It is needless to develop a list of what are our walls. We do need to do some introspection and ask forgiveness for the walls we might harbor that are not of the sort that can meet the expectations of Christian beliefs. These walls cool our relationship to God. They also are a barrier to attempting to make disciples.

We can replace our negative walls with walls of positive behavior that others can see Christ living in our actions and words.

Prayer: Father give us the faith of Nehemiah and the "can do" attitude. We give our "walls" over to you and ask forgiveness for the negativity in our lives. Amen

WEDDING AT CANA

On the third day there was a wedding at Cana in Galilee, and the mother of Jesus was there. ² Jesus was also invited to the wedding with his disciples. ³ When the wine ran out, the mother of Jesus said to him, "They have no wine." ⁴ And Jesus said to her, "Woman, what does this have to do with me? My hour has not yet come." His mother said to the servants, "Do whatever he tells you." ⁶ Now there were six stone jars there for the Jewish rites of purification, each holding twenty or thirty gallons. ⁷ Jesus said to the servants, "Fill the jars with water." And they filled them up to the brim. ⁸ And he said to them, "Now draw some out and take it to the master of the feast." So they took it. ⁹ When the master of the feast tasted the water now become wine, and did not know where it came from (though the servants who had drawn the water knew), the master of the feast called the bridegroom ¹⁰ And said to him, "Everyone serves the good wine first, and when the people have drunk freely, then the poor wine. But you have kept the good wine until now." ¹¹ This, the first of his signs, Jesus did at Cana in Galilee, and manifested his glory. And his disciples believed in him.

John 2: 1-11

Shortly after Jesus had called his disciples, we see all of them including Jesus' mother at a wedding in Cana. Jesus had just invited Nathanael to be a disciple. Nathanael became convinced of Jesus authenticity when Jesus said that he knew about Nathanael's whereabouts even before the two had met. Nathanael immediately proclaimed his belief in Jesus as being the Messiah.

At the wedding, we find Jesus together with the disciples and Jesus' mother attending. Wine was generally served at weddings in that it was a symbol of God's blessing. When the wine supply ran out, Jesus' mother notifies Jesus of the fact. Jesus addresses his mother as "Woman" which was a term of social distancing. Jesus explains that his hour of trial and crucifixion is quite distant. At this time of Jesus' ministry, he is placing emphasis on individuals privately instead of concentrating on the general public.

The miracle of changing 120 plus gallons of water into fine wine was done for a specific reason. It was the first of seven signs in the gospel of John to point specifically to Jesus as the Messiah.

For Jesus to be recognized as the Messiah was absolutely essential as a cornerstone of Jesus' ministry and the plan of salvation. In a way, this first miracle was basically Jesus' "coming out party". Just imagine the conversations among the guests wondering where this fine wine had come from. Also, just who is this Jesus?

A lesson for all of us lies in our interactions with others. None of us will attend a wedding with Jesus as a guest until the great wedding feast of the Lamb in heaven. However, as we mix with people, we just might be the only likeness of Jesus in the room.

How will we conduct ourselves? It seems that we have two choices. One choice is to do everything to blend in with the group and participate in all their secular speech and actions. Doing so, we will compromise all possibilities of a Christian witness.

Another choice is to be friends with as many as possible but to look for opportunities to let our surrounding peoples know that Jesus lives within us. Simply put, we might not ever have another time to let others know that we are believers. Jesus brought wine to the celebration to draw attention to his role as the Messiah. We bring ourselves and we bring Jesus. Are you up to it?

Prayer: Father as we associate with others, may we represent you with elegance and earnestness. Help us to be faithful witnesses. Amen

WEEDS

He put another parable before them, saying, " The kingdom of heaven may be compared to a man who sowed good seed in his field, [25] but while his men were sleeping, his enemy came and sowed weeds among the wheat and went away. [26] So when the plants came up and bore grain, then the weeds appeared also. [27] And the servants of the master of the house came and said to him, "Master did you not sow good seed in your field? How then does it have weeds?" [28] He said to them, "An enemy has done this." So the servants said to him, "Then do you want us to go and gather them? [29] But he said, "No, lest in gathering the weeds you root up the wheat along with them. [30] Let both grow together until the harvest, and at harvest time I will tell the reapers, "Gather the weeds first and bind them in bundles to be burned, but gather the wheat into my barn."

Matthew 13: 24-30

Weeds are my nemesis for not using a weed screen material after preparing a flower garden area. Many hours are spent pulling weeds and later in desperation, I apply a herbicide.

Today's parable pictures someone who was out to spoil the farmer's wheat crop. The vindictive spoiler of the wheat field probably planted darnel among the wheat. Darnel is a weedy rye that closely resembles wheat but at maturity bears small poisonous seeds.

We don't know the dynamics of what motivated someone to undermine the wheat crop. The scripture doesn't share the reason for the attempted spoiling of the wheat crop. My speculative guess is that the spoiler was probably jealous of the farmer who planted the wheat.

The wheat and the weeds were allowed to grow together because to eradicate the weeds prior to wheat harvest would do extensive damage to the wheat crop.

In our world God allows believers to mingle with unbelievers. Many sects have been formed to isolate themselves from others who do not share their belief system. Let's face it, when you isolate yourself from others who do not share your beliefs, life is much less challenging. However, one does not thrive spiritually when one is surrounded by only those that share your belief system. Christians who mix their time with unbelievers are automatically being salt and light to others. Needless to say when one interacts with non-believers, it is an opportunity to be obedient to the great commission.

Weed pulling and weed eradication has taken on a new meaning. Where are you at in your spiritual gardening?

Prayer: Father give me the desire to go and actively seek out others that could profit from my spiritual gardening methods. Amen

WEEPING

A time to weep, and a time to laugh.
Ecclesiastes 3:4

Solomon, the probable author of Ecclesiastes, states that there is a fitting time to weep as well as a time to laugh. My emotions are "worn on my sleeve" and weeping comes at times of being overwhelmed with awe in the presence of a moving testimony or musical rendition. Conversely, laughter comes quite readily also. Isn't it interesting that the creator blessed his image bearers with a full range of emotions?

Blessed are you who weep now, for you shall laugh.
Luke 6:21b

The beatitudes are comprised of blessings upon those who are already in the kingdom. I especially like the third beatitude because in it Jesus gives a special blessing upon those who weep and upon those who laugh.

But turning to them Jesus said, "daughters of Jerusalem, do not weep for me, but weep for yourselves and for your children. 29 For behold the days are coming when they will say, "blessed are the barren and the wombs that never bore and the breasts that never nursed!" 30 Then they will begin to say to the mountains, "Fall on us, and to the hills, Cover us". 31 For if they do these things when the wood is green, what will happen when it is dry.

Luke 23:28-31

Jesus, while being crucified, addresses the women in attendance and urged them to refrain from weeping for him but instead to weep for their own families. It is interesting to note that a common sentiment here on earth is to be more concerned for the generations that follow us than for our immediate needs and/or concerns.

Rejoice with those who rejoice, and weep with those who weep.
Romans 12:15

Paul in his marks of a true Christian advises us to share emotions with others in a show of harmony whether that be weeping or laughter. That is why visitation times surrounding a funeral are so meaningful. Psalm 30:5b fits in at this juncture.
Weeping may tarry for a night, but joy comes in the morning.
He will swallow up death forever and the Lord God will wipe away all tears from their faces. Isaiah 25:8b

Our eternal home will be without tears. God will wipe them away. Are you ready for a tearless eternity?

Prayer: Father, We look forward to our eternal home with you without tears of sadness. Amen

WHERE ARE YOU COMING FROM?

10 Then Moses and Aaron gathered the assembly together before the rock, and he said to them, "Hear now, you rebels: shall we bring water for you out of this rock?"
11 And Moses lifted up his hand and struck the rock with his staff twice, and water came out abundantly, and the congregation drank, and their livestock.
12 And the LORD said to Moses and Aaron, "Because you did not believe in me, to uphold me as holy in the eyes of the people of Israel, therefore you shall not bring this assembly into the land that I have given them."
13 These are the waters of Meribah, where the people of Israel quarreled with the LORD, and through them he showed himself holy.
Numbers 20: 10-13

Moses is one of the great saints of all time. Yet Moses had an attitude problem at Meribah. He showed his attitude of anger toward the Israelites in addressing them as rebels and then he hit the rock twice with his staff. Yes, water came out and the people had plenty for themselves and their livestock, but God knew Moses inner anger and temporary unbelief. So God told Moses that he would not have the honor of leading the Israelites all the way into the promised land. Moses' assistant, Joshua would have the leadership role for the remainder of the exodus. God and Moses ascended Mt. Nebo and from the mountain elevation, God showed the promised land to Moses. Moses died on that mountain at the age of 120. God buried Moses in a spot that is unknown to man.

Moses had commissioned Joshua by laying on of hands previously. This example of passing on leadership is an example of excellent planning. It would take the strong leadership of Joshua to complete the exodus.

Another lesson is that Moses, in spite of his great leadership role that communed with God on a face to face basis, was a man afflicted with original sin and only God could "read his heart".

As you analyze your own internal motivation for all of your demeanor, are you acting out of a spirit of saying thanks to God for his great plan of salvation? God knows your soul – your motivation. He knows "where you are coming from."

Prayer: I want to live a thanks filled life, Father. May my reasoning be blessed by you. Amen

WHERE ARE YOU GOING?

¹ O Lᴏʀᴅ, you have searched me and known me!
² You know when I sit down and when I rise up;
you discern my thoughts from afar.
³ You search out my path and my lying down
and are acquainted with all my ways.
Psalm 139:1-3

²³ Search me, O God, and know my heart!
Try me and know my thoughts!
²⁴ And see if there be any grievous way in me,
and lead me in the way everlasting!
Psalm 139: 23-24

Fishing is one of my passions and is readily available in the area where I live because there are many lakes and rivers. It was one of my earliest exposures to fishing when I was about five years old. In an old wooden rowboat, on a small California irrigation reservoir, with my cousin, Ed and my dad. We didn't worry about safety precautions in those early days. I stood up in the boat to attempt to land a huge bluegill, lost my balance and fell overboard. The water was about 15 feet deep and because of my swimming ability I quickly surfaced, and Ed easily hoisted me back into the boat. I recall that my dad blurted out as I was falling in "where are you going Butch?" (my nickname only used by my dad at that time).

We didn't pay attention to life jackets or boat capacity in those days. We just rented a boat, bought bait and rowed to a likely spot. By sharp contrast, we today are expected to have definable goals especially when being interviewed for another position or for a change in employer. A common question is "where do you wish to be in five years from now?"

A question that needs to be answered by everyone is "where are you going to spend eternity?" If you know for sure that you'll arrive in heaven after you die, then how are you spending your present days? Are you just waiting? Or are you living in joyous anticipation? Are you aware that Jesus has forgiven all your sins of the past, present and future? Yes Jesus died once for all the sins of everyone who is a Christian. When you consider the complete forgiveness brought about by Jesus on the cross, then doesn't it give you an absolute answer to the question we all face, "where are you going after you die?"

So where are you going? If you know that you'll be in heaven, let others know, just maybe you might be instrumental in answering the question that we all must answer "where are you going eternally?"

Prayer: Father, thank you for your saving grace that has forgiven all my sins of the past, present and future. I live in the assurance that my salvation is secure forever. Amen

WHY

[7] The end of all things is at hand; therefore be self-controlled and sober-minded for the sake of your prayers.

[8] Above all, keep loving one another earnestly, since love covers a multitude of sins.

[9] Show hospitality to one another without grumbling.

[10] As each has received a gift, use it to serve one another, as good stewards of God's varied grace:

[11] whoever speaks, as one who speaks oracles of God; whoever serves, as one who serves by the strength that God supplies—in order that in everything God may be glorified through Jesus Christ. To him belong glory and dominion forever and ever. Amen.

[12] Beloved, do not be surprised at the fiery trial when it comes upon you to test you, as though something strange were happening to you.

[13] But rejoice insofar as you share Christ's sufferings, that you may also rejoice and be glad when his glory is revealed.

[14] If you are insulted for the name of Christ, you are blessed, because the Spirit of glory[a] and of God rests upon you.

[15] But let none of you suffer as a murderer or a thief or an evildoer or as a meddler.

[16] Yet if anyone suffers as a Christian, let him not be ashamed, but let him glorify God in that name.

[17] For it is time for judgment to begin at the household of God; and if it begins with us, what will be the outcome for those who do not obey the gospel of God?

[18] And "If the righteous is scarcely saved, what will become of the ungodly and the sinner?"

[19] Therefore let those who suffer according to God's will entrust their souls to a faithful Creator while doing good.   *I Peter 4: 7-19*

"Why" is an overused word by very young children, many of whom are precocious, wanting to know how things work and why some activities are prohibited etc.

New Christians typically need to know the "whys" to be answered that pertain to what Christianity is all about. What changes should take place in one's life by becoming a Christian? If I embrace Jesus Christ as my savior, will my family and friends be okay with the decision? Once all the "whys" have been answered, the new believer prays the "Sinner's Prayer" of confession and another new person has moved toward the eternal heavenly reward.

However, as most of us have experienced, negative happenings can and do take place in the lives of both Christians and non-Christians. It is only natural for a Christian to question how bad things can happen to a Christian. After all, is not the God I worship a God of love? The simple answer to one's question of "why" really has no mortal and logical answer. Sometimes our difficulties are self-inflicted by our lifestyles. Yet that is not the ultimate answer of "why" did my God allow this severe problem to enter into my life?

So how do Christians deal with the "whys" of life? The typical problems are the death of a child or a spouse. Marital strife is another common problem, financial problems associated with pandemic fallout etc. Simply put, all of mankind faces problems that have no mortal explanation of "why" did it happen?

Some of the people react in many different ways to problems. Some are drawn closer to God in times of adversity. Their prayer lives and lifestyles becomes more God centered than was previously the case. Others draw into a cocoon type of existence and secretly blame God for allowing them to experience such a drastic turn of events. In fact such behavior, if continued for a long period of time can become a grudge against God.

The only reason that we mortals have that makes sense for our spiritual lives is that we seldom grow in our Christianity unless we are faced with problems that we can't solve readily or personally. Yes, a holy God allows bad things to happen to his children! Many times God is trying to get our attention. Our rational mindset of asking "why" for a lifetime is our attempt to have God's actions be in accordance with our expectations. If God changed according to our wishes, he would cease to be God. However, prayer does modify our experiences, but they do not replace the holiness of God.

So what is the solution to our accepting the unsolvable negatives of life? Simply put, there is no one answer. The apostle Peter in his closing statement in verse 19 advises us to entrust our souls to our faithful Creator while doing good.

J.C. Watts pastor and politician sums up the thinking on how we handle the overwhelming "whys" of life. *"It doesn't take a lot of strength to hang on. It takes a lot of strength to let go."*

Prayer: Help us to not only let go, but to also let you become the main positive in our lives. Mold us and make us after your will. Amen

WORTHY

"Don't end your life wondering why you lived". This was stated by Dr. Tony Evans, founder and senior pastor of the 10,000-member Oak Cliff Bible Fellowship in Dallas.

Wondering about our worth should be a key question in each person's life. For today's consideration, the analysis of worth falls into the areas of financial worth, societal worth and spiritual worth.

When sitting down with a financial planner, the bottom-line topic is net worth. The factors utilized in arriving at the place of "where the rubber meets the road" of financial analysis are age, present income, future expected income, debt and retirement goals. The discussion will result in current net worth and will also render a projection of financial status into retirement years.

Coupled with the facts as developed by the financial analyst could be a state of complacency when one has filled his hypothetical barns to overflowing and is building others just in case. After all you might never know. Scripture speaks to this not uncommon mindset.

The land of a rich man produced plentifully, 17 and he thought to himself, "What shall I do, for I have nowhere to store my crops?" 18 And he said, "I will do this: I will tear down my barns and build larger ones, and there I will store all my grain and my goods. 19 And I will say to my soul, "Soul you have ample goods laid up for many years; relax, eat, drink and be merry." 20 But God said to him, "Fool! This night your soul is required of you, and the things you have prepared, whose will they be?"

21 So is the one who lays up treasure for himself and is not rich toward God."

Luke 12:16b-21

Self-worth is also evaluated by our families and others in our circle of influence. Societal approval is a most cherished value for many of us. In fact it often underlines our personal feelings of self-worth. A potential problem arises when acquired wealth places an individual on a pedestal of adoration. True humility is difficult when one is idolized primarily for their net worth.

Romans 3:9-12 puts all of mankind in the same original category;

"None is righteous, no, not one; no one understands; no one seeks for God.

12 All have turned aside; together they have become worthless; no one does good, not even one."

The apostle Paul in his letter to the church at Thessalonica put things in perspective.

11 To this end we always pray for you, that our God may make you worthy of his calling and may fulfill every resolve for good and every work of faith by his power, 12 so that the name of our Lord Jesus may be glorified in you, and you in him according to the grace of our God and Lord Jesus Christ.

II Thessalonians 1: 11-12

The end result of our calling is to have so lived that Jesus Christ is glorified by our words and total demeanor. The summations of our lives are for the glory of God and him alone.

Prayer: Father as I look within myself to ascertain my worthiness, it is only through your grace that I am considered worthy through the death and resurrection of your son Jesus Christ. May my future focus be on your kingdom and may my life reflect that worthiness by your grace. Amen

YESTERDAY

Psalm 90

Lord, you have been our dwelling place
in all generations.
2 Before the mountains were brought forth,
or ever you had formed the earth and the world,
from everlasting to everlasting you are God.
3 You return man to dust
and say, "Return, O children of man!"
4 For a thousand years in your sight
are but as yesterday when it is past,
or as a watch in the night.
5 You sweep them away as with a flood; they are like a
dream,
like grass that is renewed in the morning:
6 in the morning it flourishes and is renewed;
in the evening it fades and withers.
7 For we are brought to an end by your anger;
by your wrath we are dismayed.
8 You have set our iniquities before you,
our secret sins in the light of your presence.
9 For all our days pass away under your wrath;
we bring our years to an end like a sigh.
10 The years of our life are seventy,
or even by reason of strength eighty;
yet their span[c] is but toil and trouble;
they are soon gone, and we fly away.
11 Who considers the power of your anger,
and your wrath according to the fear of you?
12 So teach us to number our days
that we may get a heart of wisdom.
13 Return, O Lord! How long?
Have pity on your servants!
14 Satisfy us in the morning with your steadfast love,

that we may rejoice and be glad all our days.
15 Make us glad for as many days as you have afflicted us,
and for as many years as we have seen evil.
16 Let your work be shown to your servants,
and your glorious power to their children.
17 Let the favor[d] of the Lord our God be upon us,
and establish the work of our hands upon us;
yes, establish the work of our hands!

Psalm 90 is a lament written by Moses. It was likely penned at the end of a laborious trek through the wilderness which lasted 38 years. The diet of the Jewish exodus people consisted of quail and manna. The desert heat was oppressive, and water was next to nonexistent. As an aside, perhaps our personal discontent with being in a state of lockdown due to the threat of the pandemic Covid-19, pales in comparison with the difficulties encountered during the exodus.

Back to the main point of today's meditation, many of us remember our yesterdays with crystal clear recall. Others might experience recalling our yesterdays because of illness and/or aging mental acuity.

Today's USA culture values speedy satisfaction. This is depicted in almost all facets of our current age. We use cell phones and computers for almost all of our communication and job performances. In fact, technology can become quickly obsolete when it is not quite as fast as other competitive brands. The emphasis is upon youth in that they keep up with technology and give the older members of society lessons on how to use the latest technology offerings.

We are so zoned into technology that a current pandemic caused lockdown, was made more bearable in that we could communicate, attend meetings including church services by sitting in our homes accessing live streaming or Zoom technology.

Could it be that we are a culture that is long on knowledge but lacking in wisdom? In other cultures, aging is revered, and their years of wisdom are utilized in future planning and decision making. The point is that those who can recall many years of yesterdays are valued.

It was common in a previous generation for aging parents to be cared for by their adult children. Some parents moved in with their children, others had their children available for meeting the necessities of life. However, our economy has so escalated that expectations derived from earning power commonly necessitate that today's wage earners consist of both spouses to work. To stay current in our fast-paced society takes a lot of money.

Nursing homes and assisted living are the current answer to what do we do with our parents that really can't handle living on their own. Many seniors are not as happy living in   such assigned circumstances because it just "isn't home".

Psalm 90 brings us back to consider our yesterdays. For those of us who have aging parents and for the parents themselves it is a comfort to hear the words of Moses when he said "God has been our dwelling place for all generations". Cultural change can't modify the eternal promises of God being the same yesterday and forever.

Even before the mountains were seen or the earth was formed our God is and has been from everlasting to everlasting.

There is no simplistic solution for dealing with our seniors. We can however set time aside to on an intentional level communicate with our parents on a more regular basis. Even though we can communicate with facetime, texts and e-mails, a phone call beats all means of keeping in touch except for a personal visit. Personal hugs and an "I love you" are irreplaceable. Also, listen to those who have been there and done that, their wisdom is based on firsthand experience and not computerized hypothetical projections.

Our prayer is taken from an old hymn:

Father we sing in our hearts
Before the hills in order stood,
Or earth received her frame,
From everlasting thou art God,
To endless years the same.
O God, our help in ages past,
Or hope for years to come,
Be thou our guide while life shall last,
And our eternal home.
Amen

Author Biography

Chuck's roots were in Redlands, California. It was a time before smog. Redlands was the navel orange capital of the USA. A truly beautiful location which featured a backdrop of mountains that were snow covered for most of the year.

Calvin College (University) was the place of college training. 1958 was the year of graduation with a degree in Education with a Biology major.

Sharon Wickstra became the reason for staying in Michigan. She became my wife and the mother of our three children. My oldest son, Mike was suddenly transported to Glory at the age of 23. My remaining children are still Michigan residents and have presented me with grandchildren and later great grandchildren. The family loves Jesus! I'm so blessed! In 2011 Sharon joined Mike in Glory. Two years later, Orlene Kuieck became my wife and filled the roles beautifully for companionship and mutual humorous "senior moments".

Two careers were in store for me. One in education with time spent in teaching, administration including the position of superintendent. Later, a second career involved group insurance programs that specialized in Michigan public schools. All my time in education and insurance were most enjoyable.

My church affiliation involved church officer duties of deacon, elder and administrative positions in Classis leadership. All the church related positions were with the Reformed Church in America.

Currently, retirement is my classification but activity is still at a very fast gait of yard grooming, symphony attendance, and time in God's beautiful outdoors in a fishing boat and occasionally in a deer blind.

Chuck Porte

Made in the USA
Monee, IL
17 August 2021

74955527R00089